KETT'S REBELLION
1549

Letting go all else, cling to the following few truths. Remember that man lives only in the present, in this fleeting instant: all the rest of his life is either past and gone, or not yet revealed. This mortal life is a little thing, lived in the corner of the earth; and little, too, is the longest fame to come - dependent as it is on a succession of fast perishing little men who have no knowledge even of their own selves, much less of one long dead and gone.
Marcus Aurelius - Meditations

By
Matthew Champion
and
Nicholas Sotherton

About the authors

Matthew Champion was born and educated in the county of Norfolk. Having worked in a variety of jobs, including pilgrim badge maker and leatherworker, he now writes full time. Specialising in historical subjects, particularly military history, he has been published in a wide variety of magazines and journals.

Previously published full length works include 'The Hollow Crown - The Story of St Edmund' which received much local acclaim from both critics and the public. Matthew is currently working on a new publication entitled 'Fortress East Anglia - 2000 years of regional defences' which is due for release in the early summer of 1999.

Nicholas Sotherton is almost as much of an enigma as Robert Kett. It is believed that he was a member of a leading Norfolk merchant family based in Norwich at the time of the rebellion and that his father, also called Nicholas, was mayor of the city in 1539. 'The Commoyson in Norfolk' appears to have been his only published work.

First published by
Timescape Publishing
The Thatched Cottage
Manor Farm
Kerdiston
Reepham
Norfolk
NR10 4RY

TIMESCAPE.CO.UK

ISBN 0 9531851 2 5

Typeset in Worcester 12pt solid

Produced and printed in England by
Albion Graphics, Norfolk.

<u>Dedication</u>

To Rebecca,
for her interest and advice

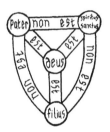

CONTENTS

Preface

Four hundred and fifty years ago East Anglia was caught up in one of the bloodiest rebellions that the region has ever witnessed. The story behind the uprising is probably one of the most fascinating accounts to have come out of the eastern counties in the last one thousand years yet few people locally know anything about it. Robert Kett and his fellow rebels helped to shape the East Anglia that we know today and played a major part in one of the great political intrigues of Tudor England yet, until very recently, Kett's rebellion has been little regarded by both historians and the public alike.

In the hot summer of 1549 a local man decided, for whatever reasons, to defy the perceived corruption of central government and stand up for the rights of the common East Anglian people. Within days thousands of people, commoners and yeomen alike, had flocked to his banners and an isolated protest had transformed itself into a full scale armed rebellion. During the uprisings short life many thousands of local men and women lost their lives and many hundreds more suffered as a result. The suppression of the revolt was both bloody and cruel and left a dark stain upon the regions history. A festering sore that was felt so deeply that for centuries it lay disregarded lest thinking of it would open all the old wounds.

This small volume, it is hoped, will go some way to remedying the situation and once more bringing the story of the rebellion to the public notice. I have attempted to write a popular history, a text that is both easily readable and enjoyable to anyone with an interest in the history of the region, and with this in mind I have included several sections of narrative that deal with events during the battle of Dussindale. These sections, although based upon true events, are simply an attempt to expand for the reader an event of which very little is actually known and perhaps give a greater understanding of the 'feel' of the period.

There are many people without whom this book would never have seen the light of day, notably: Brian Attridge (for working through the ideas with me); Chris Copage (Albion Graphics); Derek Edwards and Sue White (Norfolk Museums Service); Hugh and Priya; and most of all my wife Rebecca for her patience and understanding.

Matthew Champion, Kerdiston - January 1999

Now Syr, for the law: where is it used in England at libertie? Almost no where. The foot taketh upon him the part of the head, and commons is become a King, appointing conditions and lawes to the governours, saying 'Grant this, and that, and we will go home...'
William Paget to Protector Somerset 1549

Robert Kett of Wymondham was a traitor. With evil in his heart and the shining light of ambition in his eyes, Kett led a rebellion against his legally appointed King and the social order of the day. Robert Kett was a revolutionary intent on the destruction of Tudor society and the overthrow of the ruling class. Robert Kett was a murderer, a brigand, a thief and above all a traitor to his country. At least that is how he has been portrayed by historians until the twentieth century.

In 1949 a large stone plaque was fixed to the wall of Norwich castle. It was placed there by 'the citizens of Norwich in reparation and honour to a notable and courageous leader in the long struggle of the common people of England to escape from a servile life into the freedom of just conditions'. So, perhaps reflecting the socialist resurgence of the post war years, Robert Kett was now seen as a hero. A gentleman who stood up for the rights of the poor, the downtrodden and the socially oppressed. Not a traitor but a freedom fighter.

The truth? Well perhaps the truth lies somewhere between the two. Now, four hundred and fifty years after the rebellion, it is perhaps time to reassess the evidence, to sift through the opposing views, and draw our own conclusions. What series of events pushed so many Englishmen into open rebellion against their appointed government? Why were so many common people drawn into an uprising that led to the deaths of over three thousand of their number? Above all, who was this powerful and enigmatic leader who they willingly followed to disaster? Who was Robert Kett?

The story of Kett's rebellion is, first and foremost, an East Anglian story and although it's roots lie buried deep within the social and political events of sixteenth century England as a whole it is to East Anglia that we must look for an answer to the enigma. In 1549 England was in religious and economic turmoil. Riots were becoming commonplace and the population was almost permanently on the verge of rebellion. The commons were in belligerent mood and it needed only a small spark to ignite the tinder.

Why it was Robert Kett, a member of Norfolk's lesser gentry, who set that spark to the rebellion has always remained something of a mystery. Had Kett refused to join the rioters and stayed at home would the riot have evolved into a rebellion? Perhaps, lacking a leader, the unhappy commoners would have simply returned home themselves and continued to quietly nurse their grievances. We will probably never really know. Today all we can do is return to the earliest written records of the uprising and attempt to examine them once more. Perhaps, somewhere amongst their bias, propaganda and deliberate omissions, we may discover a clue to the true nature of the rebellion and the enigma that is Robert Kett.

Original written sources concerning the rebellion are scarce in the extreme. At such a turbulent point in England's history, few men thought to sit down and write accounts of the events they saw unfolding before them and, due to the very nature of the events themselves, all surviving accounts are written from the victors point of view. With the defeated rebels earmarked as traitors to their country, few of them are likely to have wished to draw attention to themselves.

Only two full accounts of the rebellion, written by people who either lived through it or were closely connected with it, survive to the present day. The first of these short histories, written by a gentleman called Nicholas Sotherton, is by far the most in depth and seemingly accurate account of the uprising. Although Sotherton's identity is not entirely certain, there were two Norwich citizens of that name who lived through the rebellion. It appears likely that he was the son of one Nicholas Sotherton who became Mayor of Norwich in 1539. If this Nicholas Sotherton is indeed the author of the pamphlet entitled 'The Commoyson in Norfolk' then it is likely that he knew many of the principal characters very well indeed.

Written probably within a decade of the rebellion Sotherton's text views the events very much from the point of view of the ruling class of Norwich businessmen. He has little sympathy with the rebels, as is to be expected, and is at pains to mention the many injustices suffered by the citizens at the hands of the unruly rioters. However, for all that Sotherton's account is the most detailed summary of the events that took place and, as it is written so closely to the time in question, it must be regarded as the foremost source of information concerning the rebellion in Norfolk and Norwich. Unfortunately, Sotherton's original text has not survived and we now have to rely upon a copy made either at the end of the sixteenth century or in the early years of the seventeenth century. Although this copy appears to have been a faithful reproduction of the original in almost every sense the last few pages are now missing and Sotherton's account now goes no further than the end of the battle at Dussindale.

The second full account of the rebellion, again from the point of view of the poor beleaguered citizens of Norwich, was first committed to paper in 1575, over twenty five years after the events referred to in the text actually took place. This history, written down by Alexander Neville, in many ways supports the story given by Sotherton but also sheds light upon areas that Sotherton's shorter narrative ignores. Neville was secretary to Archbishop Matthew Parker who, at the time of Kett's rebellion was serving as Vice Chancellor of the University of Cambridge and was resident in the city throughout much of the uprising. The account given by Parker to Neville obviously concentrates upon events within the city walls that actually related to Parkers activities during the troubles and although it does go into some depth concerning the causes of the uprising it also contains much that can best be described as hearsay.

Neville's account also includes several sections that include speeches reputed to have been given by Robert Kett. These speeches, although written very much with the flavour of the rebel sentiments in mind, can at best have been transcribed after the events from a third hand source as neither Parker or Neville would have been able to hear them first hand. As the actual content of these speeches does differ from the events they relate to it is best to assume that they simply grew out of a narrative need rather than any exact historical events.

These two full accounts of the rebellion are supplemented by many other sources that relate either directly or indirectly to the events in East Anglia. Of these other sources of information the most reliable, at least as far as facts, dates and figures are concerned, must be considered to be the official state papers of the reign of Edward the sixth. Although little can be found amongst the hundreds of household accounts and official correspondence that relates directly to the rebellion, what is contained within them must be considered as accurate.

Therefore if the official state papers disagree with either Neville's or Sotherton's accounts concerning such details as the number of Royal troops under Warwick's command, we must remember that the government was footing the bill and is much more likely to be correct. Other sources include many of the local parish records from the surrounding villages and the official Chamberlains record from the city of Norwich itself. Although none of these minor sources shed much light upon the overall uprising they do illuminate many minor, and hitherto overlooked, aspects of the rebellion.

However, for this work I have relied mainly upon the text of the elusive Nicholas Sotherton in his 'The Commoyson in Norfolk'. Although biased and incomplete the text was written by someone with a personal knowledge of the events and the people involved. Although I have supplemented Sotherton's work, where needed, with Neville's account it is only fitting that Sotherton should be recognised as co-author of this small work. The mistakes however, remain entirely my own.

Whereupon they fully determined removyd all that night all their ordinance and munition and all other things clene from that place they were in before, and had devised trenches and stakes wherin they and theyrs were intrenched and set up great bulwarks of defence before and abowte and placed their ordinance all abowt them and that the gentlemen the prysoners shuld not escape they take them out of theyre pryson in Surry Place and carried them to the said Dussens Dales...

Nicholas Sotherton - The Commoyson in Norfolk

As the sun rose that morning the last faint patches of smoke drifted lazily across the dew speckled grass like a fine mist. Gathering in the hollows, it spoke of a late September morning of gentle Autumn rather than the harshly heated August day that was to follow. In the distance, the city appeared in the early light, hazy beneath the dark smudge caused by the early morning cooking fires. Gradually awakening behind its breached and battered defences and overshadowed by the elegant spire of Christschurch, the townsfolk took their first accustomed glance towards the heath. Towards the rebel camp.

Last night on the heath's summit, great fires had sent their flames arrow straight into the sky. The townsfolk, remembering the night a few weeks previously when it had been their city that burnt so viciously, had locked their doors, fastened their shutters and prepared their few valuables for hasty flight. The great fires on the heath had illuminated many moving figures and the city had prepared itself for another bloody assault. Now, as light was once more restored to the scene, the soldiers guarding the city defences stared up to the heath. Towards the rebel camp.

The heath was empty. Where before it had been a straggling mass of tents and makeshift shelters it now lay desolate and ruined. As the sun rose higher the heath was laid out to view; a vast expanse of dark dusty tracks, bleached grass and smoky ruin. The camp had gone, along with the rebels, leaving nothing behind it but the few still smouldering heaps where they had torched their shelters before moving on. The bleached grass rectangles showed where the tents had stood amidst the hovels and spidery dark lines still marked where tracks and roads had run towards the great oak at its centre. Now the heath lay bare beneath the warming sun like a ghostly map laid flat upon the Norfolk landscape. A bleached and smoking echo from the past.

News of the rebels departure moves hastily through the city as messengers speed from the fortifications into the maze of tangled streets. Officers climb the Cathedral tower and strain their eyes against the newly risen sun. As the word spreads the townsfolk, some bewildered, some angry, leave their homes and gather by the river, and at the ruined and shattered city gate, to stare at the empty camp. The crowd spreads along the rivers bank flowing around the now silent guns that stand starkly entrenched behind their low earth ramparts. Some are shouting, others laughing. A holiday atmosphere betrays the few darkly sullen individuals who regret the rebels passing. The mood is broken by the sharp sound of horsemen in the cobbled city streets.

From around the high walls of the cathedral hasten twenty or so mounted soldiers clattering through the tidal ebb and flow of the crowd. These men, grim set faces beneath bright steel helmets, bellow at the crowd for passage. The townsfolk draw back chastened by the harsh guttural commands of the German cavalry and the horsemen pass swiftly through the shattered gateway. Putting their horses to the slope the cavalry are soon out of sight as they pass up among the scrubby trees and climb towards the heath. The clamour quietens as the townsfolk lose sight of the mounted hunters. These lance knights who fight only for money and know not friend from foe, send a shiver of mistrust through all but the hardest hearts.

The horsemen appear a few minutes later among the broken ruin of the rebels camp. They draw rein by the great oak tree before splitting into groups and spreading out towards the east. Spurring forwards they canter off into the sunrise to search out their prey. To find the rebels.

The rising sun begins to heat the early morning air into a glittering shimmer that obscures the now deserted rebel camp. The early dew, so sweet for the long parched grass of this oven like summer, evaporates into the early morning and leaves the expectation of another iron hot day. When the horsemen return via the Bishops bridge and its battered gateway less than an hour later, there are few there to meet them. The gunners, grateful for the respite from the rebel bombardment, lay slouched amongst the tools of their trade and eye the approaching horsemen warily. The gun captain from the Cow tower has wandered in the early warmth along the river bank. His beleaguered outpost, built to defend the northeastern corner of the city, had only yesterday been almost cut off by the rebels and their withdrawal has come as a blessed relief. In this heat the tower was no place to be shut up with twenty burly gunners, and he breathes the warm air with deep satisfaction. He reaches the shot battered gate-house at the Bishops bridge just as the first half dozen of the German horsemen clatter excitedly to a halt. They have found the rebels.

A bare two miles to the east the great rebel force has assembled itself in the warming sun of this late summer morning. Moving their camp under cover of darkness they have found a new position where they can make their stand. In the open ground of the wide heath the rebels have drawn up their lines to await the coming of the soldiers. They know the soldiers will come. They understand now that there must be a resolution to this long drawn out dispute. The men are quiet as they prepare their new defences. Spades dig deep into the hard, sun baked ground and breath comes too short for idle chatter. They know the soldiers will come. Few of them now regret their actions over the past months. They had a point to make, believed they were standing up for the young King's wishes, and now betrayed upon all sides they will stand and make their final protest together. They work fast to be ready for the soldiers.

Few of them now believe that there will be much of a fight. They will listen to the heralds, take the token offers that will undoubtedly be made and then disband their army and return home. As the ditches are deepened and the banks raised, a few voices still chew over old arguments only to be shouted down by Miles the gunner as he redirects his workmen to their task. Miles, the staunchest ally of the rebel leaders, feels uneasy as he studies the new, half finished, fortifications. No one really believes that there will be a battle but Miles has a strange feeling that all will not go to plan. Ever glancing to the dark smudge in the west that marks the city he bellows at his men to redouble their efforts. He wants to be ready when the soldiers come. Ready for anything.

At about an hour before noon the rebel look-outs, placed well to the west over looking the city, begin to return to the new camp. The Royal army is on the move and the soldiers are coming. The few remaining rebel watchers posted near the city can now clearly see the soldiers advance. From the north, bright sunlight glinting on helmets, spears and halberds, the Kings troops emerge from the crowded streets of Norwich. As they appear from the gates they turn east to follow the river. Passing the bend in the bright ribbon of the river Wensum a ragged cheer issues forth from the now relaxing gunners in the Cow tower. From their battered embrasures the gunners watch the soldiers pass and chatter to each other like excited children. A holiday atmosphere with a parade to match.

First come the grim faced German cavalry, their doublets showing gaudy and bright beneath their polished steel, short lances raised aloft in answer to the cheer. They know their task and though fighting only for money they know they are good at their jobs. To rout a gaggle of peasants is nothing more than a gentle morning exercise to these veterans. Then come the loyal local lads, drab as hens next to their peacock foreign cousins, but with their bows strung tight and full, goose fletched shafts stuffed in their belts, determined not to sell themselves short before such a brave company. Caught up in their own dignity they cast quick sidelong glances at the now waving gunners and grin nervous smiles. Behind them, amongst the quality, come the sombre faces of Captain Drury's handgunners. Dour professionals they march past the tower with barely a glance at the antics of their amateur counterparts. Their matches lit they go to revenge themselves on rebel knaves and yet they doubt they'll fight.

The line of men, all armed and geared for war, takes the Yarmouth road and heads towards the east. The sun is almost at its zenith and the dust flies up to irritate already parched throats. Gradually the marching line disappears and the Cow tower gunners return to their own amusing tasks, each glad to be shaded and cool and not out there sweating in the heat. A long, dusty, sweat stained march is one thing they could do without. After all, the rebels will not fight.

The rebels watch the soldiers march. They see the clouded dust rise like fine smoke above the line of march and know that an army comes against them. Spades and mattocks drive hard into the baked soil to finish their work before the soldiers come. Half finished bulwarks litter the plain and where a forest of sharpened stakes should stand only a few deadly coppices appear. Miles swears under his breath and then swears louder still at his workmen. Wiping his sweaty forehead upon his doublet sleeve, he glances to the west once more and sees the glint of sun on armour. A few minutes longer and his men must take their positions. Behind half finished defences they must face down an army. Miles swears again. Turning his back on the advancing cavalry as they spread out across the plain, Miles stalks off to find his beloved guns. Those around him can still hear him swearing beneath his breath.

To the west the Royal army, now within sight of the rebel positions, begins to deploy itself for battle. The German cavalry, kicking their already sweating mounts into a canter, leave the hard packed surface of the road and spread out across the plain like a long dammed stream breaking its banks. Their flags, bright against the bleached landscape, mark their gaudy progress as they wheel away to the north. Well trained and steady they bring their horses to order and form up in two brightly coloured echelons that flank the rebels position. More slowly now the gap between the two begins to fill. The Royal footsoldiers, secure between the horsemen file into their allotted positions. Gradually, beneath the mixed and coloured banners, the army forms into a tight packed wall of glinting weapons. As the commanders gallop their horses along the lines, urging here and coaxing there, the last of the Royal army moves to its allotted site.

Trundling east, on screeching and complaining axles, come the Royal guns. Amidst the swearing and sweating of the Welsh wagoners the sleek bronze cannons, newly cast with virgin barrels, swing off the road onto the rough ground of the dale. Now the mules, fatigued by heat and the dust of the armies trail, twitch their ears as the closeness of the Germans horses revive their flagging spirits. The Welshmen, dark surly rogues with no good word to say for this eastern land, take their time to quieten the troubled beasts. Their embarrassment and mistakes forgotten the Welsh drive the guns forward through the lines with new found pride as the army looks on. With unlooked for haste the sleek death dealing monsters are unhitched and turned to face the dark smear to the east that is the rebel army. The soldiers, Welsh, English and German, have come to Dussindale.

Silence now falls on Dussindale. The Royal army, drawn up in all its splendour, sits passively beneath the hot sun awaiting its orders. In the centre, behind the dotted line of cannon, Captain Drury paces between the stretched lines of his hackbutters. He knows that most of the footsoldiers have been left in the city and that his company, his most professional of units, his pride and his joy, will take little part in whatever is to come. Yet still he paces, unable to relax as the men about him do, and worries about what the day will bring. Bright movement catches his eye and, halted in his endless progress up and down, he turns to watch as two horsemen gallop through the lines.

The rebels watch the horsemen's slow approach as they gallop across the bare ground between the two armies. Dust kicks up from the heels of the beasts as they cross a dry trackway and the sun, reflecting from the armour of the riders, sends bright patches of light to play upon the great banner that streams out behind them in the lifeless air. In the stillness that pervades the field it seems to take an age for the horsemen to reach the rebel lines. These two specks, the only movement on a field of calm.

The rebels, sensing the importance of the moment, stiffen at the horsemen's approach. Miles, bent double and busy preparing his gritty powder charges, glances up as the horses slow to a trot near one of his guns. He sees the younger of the two men stare at the long bronze beast that sits sullen in the dry grass and grimaces. Miles allows himself a sly grin, whether it is the menacing air of the recumbent cannon or the Royal cipher upon its tapered barrel that unsettles, he is satisfied with the effect. From the top of his long riding boot, the older of the two horsemen, pulls a thickly folded sheet of paper, smooths it flat upon his beasts neck and glancing nervously round at the upturned wary faces, begins to read.

Resigned, Miles leans over the long sun warmed barrel of the cannon and listens to the Royal proclamation. The long wordy preamble drones on and Miles' mind begins to wander. Men around him shuffle their feet, anxious to get to the meat of the matter and stare upwards at the sun reddened faces of the couriers. The monotonous drone continues, interrupted only by the readers attempt to swat a fly, drawn by the sweaty horses, that buzzes around his head. The rebels, finding the monologue more tedious than an Easter mass, begin to mutter good naturedly among themselves. The Royal courier, sensing the disquiet pauses to glance around him and then launches, with undisguised ferocity, into the last part of his message. Surrender and their lives may be spared, defy the Royal authority and die like the dogs they are.

To a man the rebels stand, stunned by the wording of the announcement, and stare at the now satisfied countenance of the courier. His comrade, feeling the tension, glances quickly over his shoulder at the reassuring bulk of the Royal army. Miles, now standing ramrod straight by his cannon, feels almost light-headed. Fighting hard to keep his temper he stares at the horsemen. They, all three, can sense the change in the crowds mood. Loyal goodwill has turned to a stunned belligerence and here and there men take a pace or two forward as if to seize the messengers. Mutters and growls grow in volume to a high incoherent roar of defiance. The moment of peace is lost and the bellow of the crowd shatters more than quiet. Peace itself lies shattered.

In a moment the horsemen are away. Wheeling their mounts and raking their sweaty flanks with their spurs they launch into a gallop that will take them to the safety of their own lines. Behind them they leave an angry mob. Miles, his initial irritation cooling, can feel only a sense of loss and foreboding. Where a few kind words would have had the rebels moist eyed and vowing allegiance to their sovereign the messengers speech has created a resolute enemy. A dispute that would have been best resolved over a mug of ale would now end in bloodshed. Bitter and anxious Miles takes up the first of his powder charges and, with heavy heart, begins to load his cannon.

Captain Drury, in the centre of the Royal line, hears the rebels shout and stiffens. This is not the joyous yell of relief from newly pardoned men but rather a scream of hatred and defiance. Staring through the heat shimmering distance of the plain he can make out the hasty return of the two horsemen. Their flight, run ragged by its unseemly haste, speaks louder than the noise of the rebels and raises a guttural laugh from several of the German horsemen. Around him Drury senses that his men understand. Matches are blown into glowing embers, weapons checked and swords loosened in scabbards. With a resigned sigh Drury prepares himself for what is to come. Against all odds the rebels are going to fight.

Within the rebel army all is now determined and hasty movement. Miles, his half score of cannon now safely loaded, stands stiff by his powder store and watches all that goes on around him. Resigned now to the fight he eyes the enemy with an experienced eye, judging their strengths and weaknesses. Through the heat shimmer he can see the additional haze caused by the smoke from the many hundreds of lit slowmatches and tries to judge their numbers. The rebel army is almost twice the size of their Royal opposition yet Miles knows the shortcomings of raw troops in their first battle. Trying not to allow his concern to show on his face he wanders the length of his guns giving reassurance to his nervous gun captains and sharing a joke or two with the men. They are in defiant mood. The rebels are going to fight.

From Miles's left, among the sheep folds by the Yarmouth road, a small procession winds itself through the rebel position. Miles stares as they approach the front of the rebels defences. Three men on horseback followed by a gaggle of men on foot. The three leaders, recognising the burly gunner, each raise their hands in turn and draw their little procession to a halt. Miles knows these men well, the leaders of the rebellion, they form an unholy Trinity that he muses may just have led them all to destruction. As the three dismount Miles shrugs and turns back to the complex task of sighting his guns. Whatever the three men want matters very little to him now. They have said more than enough already. Miles edges the trail of his largest cannon a little to the left to line its bleak muzzle with the distant Royal standard and crouches to sight along the dull sheen of the bronze barrel.

With his deadly charges now truly sighted Miles straightens and turns his eye upon his leaders. Time has almost run its course. The end of this act, be it farce or tragedy is fast approaching and Miles simply awaits the final signal. The simple nod or quiet word that will begin this last bloody act and let loose the horror that is civil war.

The little procession moves off once more and makes to pass through the rebel lines. In its wake, left chained and stiff upon the sun bright plain stand a dozen or so men. These prisoners of the rebellion, the cause of so much unjust dispute, now stand between the two armies. Chained to the sharpened stakes that mark the rebels front they hang from their shackles, a dozen pale and quaking men. Imprisoned by the rebels for their numerous crimes, be they greed, inhumanity or simple selfishness, these few must now watch the final act played out before their eyes. These scum, whose hatred has brought death in its wake, must now stand impotently by and watch their own deaths charge across the plain. Miles hears a sharp and bitter laugh echo along the now silent rebel lines and to his surprise he finds it coming from his own dry throat.

Once more silence settles on Dussindale. Two great forces stand opposed across the glorious sunlit plain and wait for the killing to begin. Two armies, both claiming loyalty to the same young boy who is their King, prepare to kill each other in the hot summer sunshine. Miles pours a meagre pile of fine powder into the touch hole of his beloved cannon. A minute quantity hardly enough to make a spark yet enough to begin the slaughter. In the distance the cavalry begin to stir, the word is shouted from the rear and Miles leans towards his charge. As the slowmatch fires the priming, Miles steps back and watches with a casual air as the force of the charge erupts. Mouth open to stop his eardrums bursting he watches as his charge rockets backwards speeding iron death towards the advancing Royal troops. As the first shots, perfectly aimed, strike home the Royal standard flutters to the ground and Miles mutters 'Sweet Jesu, protect us'.

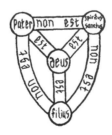

Upon occasion that by a commandment from the Prince upon complaint made for enclosing of divers common grounds that divers commissioners upon view therof by a day should have done, and for not doeing therof, was in Norfolk a rumour that in Kent and other places divers that had laid open, percieving many others did not the same, and therfore thought good of theyre own authority to lay those grounds open also.
Nicholas Sotherton - The Commoyson in Norfolk

The year of our Lord 1549, third year of the reign of his most glorious majesty King Edward the sixth, was a year of blood and rebellion. Throughout that long hot summer the disputes and grievances of half England boiled to the surface and erupted into violent revolt. By high summer half the population of England was either in open rebellion or muttering darkly of ancient grudges and unfulfilled promises. The government of the realm, entrusted during the young King's minority to a council of state, was tearing itself apart through internal strife and law and order was near to general breakdown. Two Royal armies, led by the nobility of England, stood to arms and general civil war looked to be only a few short weeks away.

To discover the reasons behind this complex slide towards general anarchy we must first look at the tangled political and social history of the preceding years of Edward's troubled reign. King Edward's father, Henry VIII, died on January 28th 1547 at the age of fifty six having reigned for over thirty seven years. He left behind him only one sickly son and a realm that on the surface appeared calm and stable, At the age of eight Edward found himself King of England and master of one of Europes greatest evolving monarchies.

However, all was not as well with the young Kings realm as it at first appeared. His fathers split with the Roman church, his confiscation of church lands and subsequent dissolution of the monastery system had caused much general disquiet within the population and coupled with his advance of agricultural reforms and increased taxation Henry left a country in which a large part of the common folk felt general disaffection. However, Edward, at the tender age of eight, was not going to be the man who would have to face the wrath of the people. That was left for his councillors.

In Henry's will he had decreed that during the young King's minority the actual work of the day to day government should be undertaken by a council of ministers. The council was to consist of sixteen equal ministers, whom Henry named, and who all either owed their advancement or their titles to the late King. No single member of the council was to be dominant and all were to share in equal power until the young Edward was of an age to take the reins of government himself. The late King, aware as he was of at least some of the troubles he had stored up for his son, made a point of creating a council that reflected the religious and political make up of the nation. Alongside Protestant reformers he appointed conservative Catholics, and older statesmen were balanced by younger dynamic men of action. Unfortunately, for both Henry and the country as a whole, even such a well laid plan must rely upon the vagaries of men; men of ambition.

Even as the old King lay dying his plan was falling apart. In the corridors about the palace of Westminster members of the council in waiting were conspiring together to override the orders contained in the will. By the time of Henry's death Edward Seymour, Earl of Hertford had already gained the support of the councils most powerful members to declare himself Lord Protector of the realm during the new Kings minority.

Edward Seymour was a typical product of his time. Born in 1505 Edward was the eldest son of Sir John Seymour of Wolf Hall in Wiltshire and upon the death of his father in 1536 he inherited one of the largest estates in that county. The marriage of his sister Jane to the young King Henry in the same year obviously elevated his standing at court but as a competent soldier, having served successfully in both France and Scotland, he had already attracted the martial eye of the King. However, unlike so many relations of Henry's wives who achieved initial advancement, Edward retained his Royal patronage even after the death of his sister Jane in 1537. Made Knight of the Garter in 1541 and commander of the English forces in the wars of 1543-6, he achieved considerable personal popularity both at court and, more surprisingly, among the commoners. As uncle to the young King Edward, Seymour appeared as the obvious choice to oversee his minority.

This move by Seymour, soon to promote himself to Duke of Somerset, cannot be simply viewed as the rapid seizure of power by a graspingly ambitious noble. Somerset, as he was know known, did not have to force or coerce the other council members into this action, they joined in his plot freely, and all felt that it would be in the nations interest. Since the rise of the Tudors to the throne England had experienced a period of internal stability that after the half century of strife known as the Wars of the Roses had come as a blessed relief. This stability was the result of the strong and personal government of Henry VIII and his father Henry VII and faced now with a child as King the nobility feared that the power vacuum would lead to a return to factional disorder. Somerset, acting with the support of the majority of the council, believed that he could fill the vacuum and maintain the peace. In this, however, he was sadly mistaken.

The problems that had arisen and festered under the strong and disciplined rule of Henry VIII were always going to be a source of trouble for his successor. No matter how strong the leadership a point would eventually be reached when the mutterings of disquiet would turn into howls of dissent. Unfortunately, at least for Somerset, the appearance of a pseudo monarch, in the shape of a Lord Protector, was just the spark that was needed to ignite the powder keg of discontent. Whereas a King ruled by right of succession and divine authority, a Protector was no more than an ambitious nobleman with all the worries, cares and faults of a commoner.

The two areas of general discontent in various strata of the population that were to play such a crucial role in the events of 1549 both had their roots in changes either introduced or encouraged by Henry VIII. The first, the religious reformation, was almost wholly the responsibility of the former King, and although playing little or no part in the events in East Anglia it did directly and indirectly effect the outcome of events. The second area, that of the enclosure of common land, had been an ongoing process for many decades. The fact that it played such a major part in the development of Kett's rebellion simply shows that it had begun to reach a level that, combined with other financial and agricultural factors, adversely affected the lot of the common agricultural worker and yeoman farmer.

In the century or so leading up to the unrest in 1549 enclosure had been a common subject of popular discontent. Although in its most harmless form, being the redistribution of manorial lands to create larger and more efficient individual holdings, it was generally accepted as being beneficial. Enclosure was simply one step in a long process of agricultural reform that would eventually lead to the loss of the commons land and the subsequent suffering of the poorer classes. This enclosure of common land by the lord of the manor and the introduction of larger estate farms did of course mean the destruction of the smaller tenant farms. Whereas the old manorial system had assured everyone of both their rights and their responsibilities the new system meant not only the loss of tenants rights but in many cases their land as well.

As is so commonly the case in such reforms the enclosure of land was profit led.

Any farmer who, realising that the redistribution of his many small manorial holdings into one larger area meant greater efficiency and subsequently larger profits, would soon begin to look to acquire further land to add to his holding and increase his profit still further. In many cases, with the destruction of the manor system, it was possible to buy or rent extra acreage and soon enough greedy eyes were turned upon the common land. For many of the smaller farmers the common land that they had access to meant the difference between survival and starvation. Without it they did not have enough land to sustain themselves or their families. It was at this point, with the increasing enclosure of the commons, that the already poor farmer would begin to find himself squeezed still further. As many of these poorer farmers did not actually own their own land, rather holding it as tenants or copyholders from the manor, they soon found that along with the loss of common land their own farms were being sold out from under them.

East Anglia, with its vast tracts of common land was particularly susceptible to the threat of enclosure. With the rise of the English wool and cloth market, in which East Anglia played a considerable part, enclosed land became desperately sought by the larger farmers and nobility who wished to keep sheep. The keeping of large flocks of sheep on enclosed land was particularly resented by the poorer classes. Not only did it deprive them of what was once common grazing but it also meant that large areas of land could be farmed with minimal overheads and few supervising labourers. Where before a dozen men farmed, now a single shepherd gathered his flock. Eventually resentment led to violence and the pulling down of enclosure fences becomes one of the most frequently found offences in local riots.

Lord Protector Somerset, unlike the great majority of his class, seems to have actually understood and sympathised with the views of those who opposed enclosure. Although personally opposed to unfair enclosure causing families to starve and farmers to look to the poor rate for support, Somerset's real opposition stemmed from a far different source.

In the years leading up to the rebellions of 1549 England had witnessed, for the first time, inflation on a modern scale. Since the turn of the century it has been estimated that prices more than doubled. Had this been a steady rise of a few percent per annum it is likely that although troublesome the rise in prices would not have become a major problem for the administration, however, the level of inflation rose dramatically in about 1542 and remained unnaturally high for nearly a decade. The reasons behind this sudden and unexpected increase are still a little unclear to this day. No doubt the crippling cost of the foreign wars that so marked Henry VIII's later reign were in part responsible and the subsequent sale of crown lands and debasement of the coinage only added to its effect. However, Somerset, along with several other learned gentlemen of the period, laid the blame fairly and squarely at the door of sheep farming and enclosures.

Somerset believed, be it rightly or wrongly, that the increase in sheep farming and its subsequent rise of enclosures, lessened the amount of land under arable agriculture. Coupled with a dramatic rise in the general population and the appalling droughts of the early 1540's, this created a shortage of foodstuffs that led to higher prices and overall inflation. To Somerset the answer seemed simple. Tight restrictions upon the number of enclosures allowed would keep land under tillage and therefore gradually reduce inflation. In the eyes of the common people Somerset, already popular, became the 'Good Duke'.

Lord Protector Somerset's policies concerning, what he considered, the harm being done by general enclosure were two fold. Firstly, and regarding the rebellions of 1549, most importantly Somerset took a very lenient line when it came to disorders that stemmed from enclosure. Rioters began to find that their actions of pulling down fences were, if not tolerated, looked upon with sympathy. In May 1548 Somerset granted a pardon to rioters in the turbulent county of Cornwall who had risen up in the closing months of the old King's reign to protest against the enclosure of the commons. In the months that followed, other pardons were granted as riots against enclosure spread throughout the nation and petitions lodged in the Court of Requests against new enclosures were often upheld.

This lenience and support of the common man may have endeared Somerset to the general population but it was certainly not looked upon with favour by his fellow councillors. Many of them believed, quite rightly, that this lenience would not only alienate many members of the gentry but also encourage further unrest amongst the commoners. It has been suggested many times since that it was Somerset's failure to take a harsh line against these smaller civil disorders that convinced the leaders of Kett's rebellion that they would not only be tolerated by the Protector but actually receive his support.

The second main area of Somerset's policies concerned the actual creation of the hated enclosures. Believing that tighter controls would result in fewer enclosures and therefore lower inflation Somerset instituted the establishment of various commissions. The commissions were divided into smaller committees whose task was to survey the country, county by county, and prepare a report upon the state of enclosure. These reports were then to be put before a new Parliament so that they might create legislation designed to counter the enclosure movement. The committees were also to inquire into specific cases of unlawful enclosure which could then be acted against in the courts.

Although these seeds of reform appear, at least on paper, to have begun to address the many problems thrown up by enclosures in actuality very little real change occurred. Only one committee, that for the midland shires, ever actually got as far as taking the road, and it was forced to disband by its members who had other business to attend to, long before its findings were in any form to be presented to Parliament.

In fact, had Somerset's policies ever been given the chance of reaching fruition it is likely that very few changes would have been able to be implemented. The cloth industry, blamed by so many for the increase of the enclosures, had by this time just about reached its natural peak. The need for enclosure for sheep farming was diminishing and the dramatic rise of the enclosure of the common lands had also reached its peak. The damage had, in effect, already been done.

However, the people of England were not to know this at the time. They saw Somerset's policies as backing for their dramatic actions against enclosure and believed that they were actually helping Somerset's reforms to take effect. Civil disorders and riots began to spread throughout the length and breadth of England, as the commons rose up to throw down the fences. Events were moving faster than any possible reforms and in the spring of 1549 they finally got out of control. In both Cornwall and East Anglia law and order collapsed and civil unrest blossomed into armed rebellion.

I told your Grace the truth, and was not believed: well, now your Grace seithe it what seythe your Grace? Mary, the King's subjects owt of all discipline, owt of obedience, caryng neither for Protector nor King, and much lesse for any other meane officer. And what is the cause? Your own levytie, your softness, your opinion to be good to the poor. I knowe, I say, your good meaning and honest nature. But I saye, Syr, yt is a great pity (as the common proverbe goeth in a warm summer) that ever fayre weather should do harm.
William Paget to Protector Somerset - 7th July 1549

By the spring of 1549 the fact that some sort of civil unrest would strike the English countryside during the summer months had become almost inevitable. Events had stolen a march upon policies and it would have taken a wiser and more far sighted politician than Somerset to quell the discontent. However, the fact that these outpourings of resentment transformed themselves into not one, but two, fully fledged and armed uprisings can only reflect badly upon the administration of the day. The first of the powder kegs to ignite was Cornwall.

Throughout the country during the spring and early summer of 1549 riots and disturbances became almost a commonplace event. In towns and villages throughout the land the commoners, seeing the Protectors sympathy towards their complaints, took to the fields to pull down the hated enclosure fences. Landowners were set upon and the politics of the mob ruled the day. However, though no doubt aggrieved by the rise of enclosures, it was quite a different matter that finally, at the beginning of June, drove the Cornish commoners into rebellion.

The previous two years had been troubled and violent times in the normally peaceful county of Cornwall and these troubles can be laid fairly and squarely at the door of one man, William Body, government agent for the county. Body, an unpopular, unscrupulous and ambitious careerist, had been charged by the authorities with implementing the Edwardian religious reformation within the county. His brutal handling of an obviously tense and sensitive situation can be held responsible for much of the trouble that was to follow. Had Body possessed a sweeter nature or been a better judge of the popular mood then it is likely that, as in the majority of the country, bloodshed could have been avoided.

Trouble really began to brew upon Body's return to Cornwall in 1547. He had already caused general ill feeling and anger over his handling of the collection of funds from the archdeaconry of Cornwall, a position he had acquired from Thomas Wolsey's illegitimate son in exchange for an outstanding debt. After successfully defeating the Bishop of Exeter's challenge to his rights to collect money, Body had left the county in relative peace for six years. His return to the area as government agent not only reopened many of the old wounds but also created much new hostility.

Body's return to Cornwall was the result of him being created government agent for the region with the task of overseeing the religious changes that were taking place throughout England. Conservative Cornwall, already aggrieved by the governments unsympathetic handling of the situation, took the opportunity to make their grievances known. Body had been charged with ensuring that the inventories being compiled by government commissioners upon the remaining religious foundations in the county were carried out to the letter. Whether from wickedness or just plain insensitivity Body gave the impression that these inventories were to be a precursor to the confiscation of the church goods being surveyed. The commons, ever protective of their favoured institutions, reacted violently and riots ensued. The government, worried about the effect of a western rising, dealt leniently with the trouble makers and attempted to patch up the deteriorating situation.

The following year, 1548, Body once more returned to Cornwall on government business. This time his task was to ensure that the new laws concerning the destruction of religious images in churches were being carried out. Once more his less than tactful approach to the problem created hostility wherever he went. Finally, arriving at Helston, he was met by an angry mob who, led by the rebellious parish priest of St Keverne, attacked and killed him. The government, panicked by this blatant murder of one of their officers, sent out commissions for the raising of troops to put down what they feared could escalate into an open rebellion. Luckily the death of the hated Body seemed to appease the disgruntled commoners and, perhaps fearing the government response, they peacefully returned to their homes.

The government's actual response to the outrage of Body's murder was perhaps typical of the period. With the unpopular Body dead and the majority of the religious changes already instituted, Somerset and the council decided to take a sympathetic view of the situation and, rather than antagonise the rebels and risk further violence, a general pardon was issued to all except the ringleaders. Of these twenty eight trouble-makers only ten were eventually brought to justice and hung for their crime, once again giving the rioters the impression that they had the tactic support of the authorities. The council, and Somerset in particular, rather than defusing a tense situation were simply storing up trouble for themselves in the years to come.

The final spark that ignited the Cornishmen's already short fuse and transformed the many localised disturbances into a full blown armed rebellion came in the early summer of 1549. Throughout the county rumours began to spread that the new simplified church liturgy, published in the new Edwardian book of common prayer, was to be introduced on Whitsunday. Outraged at the insensitivity of the authorities and wishing to make their feeling known the commoners of the Bodmin area joined together to protest. Under the leadership of one Humphrey Arundel, a well known local trouble maker and rabble rouser, the rebels converged on the town of Bodmin and there established a camp. It was from this camp, under the guidance of a collection of traditionalist priests, that the rebels issued their first set of demands.

Seen in the light of later events the actual demands put forward by the rebels are extremely straightforward. They wished for the continuance of their religious observances in the form that tradition had passed down to them. The new liturgy seemed to them as little more than a 'Christmas game' and they wanted nothing to do with it. For them religion should be practised as it had always been done and no commands from central government could change their minds. It is also an interesting reflection on the insular state of England at the period that the Cornishmen demanded for the mass to be said in Latin rather than English because 'certen of us understande no Englysh'. However, no matter how reasonable the demands of the rebels appear to modern eyes they proved to be completely unacceptable to the strongly Protestant views that predominated in London.

It must be understood that the changes that were being implemented in the Church were, in the eyes of many, unacceptably radical. Although it was during the reign of Henry VIII that the split away from the church of Rome had actually taken place and the acts for the suppression of the monasteries had been passed the daily nature of the church services had remained essentially catholic. Now, under the rule of the Protestant reformers, all that was being changed. Edward's new book of common prayer, issued at Easter 1549, outlawed many of the old and well respected acts of worship of the church. Pilgrimage was banned, the lighting of candles for individual saints was discontinued, numerous religious festivals were removed from the calendar and the mass was now to be said in English rather than Latin. Coupled with the general attacks upon what the reformers viewed as 'superstition' the new prayer book outlined a radical change in the way the common people of England practised their faith.

From the camp at Bodmin the rebels, leaving a small force to loosely blockade the still loyal port of Plymouth, began their march into Devon. Gathering support along the line of their march the Cornishmen were joined by rebels from Devon who had risen up independently from the Cornish uprising. Once again the introduction of the new prayer book had caused the ill feeling to boil into action and by the 20th of June a combined force of some 20,000 rebels was encamped at the small town of Crediton.

It was while the rebel army was encamped at Crediton that the government made their first real attempt to disperse the angry gathering. Sir Peter Carew, a former High Sheriff of Devon, was ordered to the area by the council with orders to try and pacify the rebels. Once again the government, in its choice of an officer to talk to the rebels, had made a stupid and simple mistake. Carew as a well known and radical Protestant, was probably one of the men least suited to suppressing a strongly conservative Catholic mob.

On the 21st of June Carew, after consulting with the local gentry at Exeter, rode the few miles to Crediton to meet with the rebels. Accompanied by a small unit of soldiers he arrived at the town to find it well defended and swarming with, by now, armed and resentful rebels. Attempts to open a dialogue with the rebel leaders failed even before they got started and, for reasons unknown, one of Carew's men took it upon himself to set fire to some of the buildings that formed part of the rebels fortifications. A bad situation was now out of hand, and the rebels, in the panicked belief that this fire heralded a major attack, deserted the town. Carew, confronted by a countryside full of hostile rebels, quickly withdrew. The rebels, by now convinced that the authorities were out to completely destroy them, regrouped and moved on Exeter.

The rebels, now in a highly belligerent and volatile mood, established a new camp at Clyst St Mary, a village a few miles east of Exeter, and from where they could block the London road. Fresh attempts were now made to open negotiations and two local gentlemen, Sir Thomas Denys and Sir Hugh Pollard, were allowed to enter the camp. Sympathising with the rebels demands Denys and Pollard managed to convince them that their best option lay, not in open rebellion, but rather in a lawful petition to the council. However, on their return to Exeter Carew, never given to diplomatic niceties, claimed that this advance was by no means enough and even hinted that both Denys and Pollard were in league with the rebels. Disillusioned with the lack of solid progress from the negotiations and heartened by the local authorities apparent internal divisions the rebels now took the dramatic and fateful step of actually laying siege to the city.

Meanwhile, in London, the council were virtually unaware of the rapid and tempestuous events taking place around Exeter. With limited communications and enclosure riots taking place closer to home in the midlands the council found both their time and resources very limited. Fearing both a Scottish and French invasion the Protector had few troops to spare for what still appeared to him as a very limited uprising. It was only the arrival in London of Carew, dishevelled from days of hard riding after escaping the siege at Exeter, that finally brought home to the Protector the dangerous proportions now reached by the western rebellion.

Finally, with the possible threat of a march against London, the council acted against the western rebels. Dispatching Lord Russell to take command of the dangerous situation the council was only capable of supplying him with a small and totally inadequate number of troops. With threats in both the north and the south the council felt that they could not provide any extra men for fear of weakening their other defences and anticipated Russell being able to boost his force by enlisting troops along the way. However, with both Somerset and Wiltshire sympathetic to the rebels, recruits were not forthcoming and Russell, hopelessly outnumbered and with little support from London, found it impossible to advance to the aid of Exeter.

Faced by a massive rebel force and unsure of the loyalties of even the countryside through which he marched Russell had little choice but to attempt to contain the situation and stop the rebellion spreading. Fearing a general march on London Russell simply sat in the path that the rebels would have to take just to the east of Honiton. Being unable to advance due to lack of troops and unable to retire due to political pressure Russell had no option but to remain where he was; in limbo. Finally, after several desperate appeals to the council Somerset, on July 10th, allowed Russell more troops with which to end the rebellion.

Now, in the second week in July, with the French and the Scots threatening the borders, riots in the midlands and south east and a major rebellion in the west Somerset's position looked very precarious. The forces loyal to the Crown, already supplemented by foreign mercenaries, were stretched dangerously thin. Extra reinforcements intended for Lord Russell and the western campaign had to be diverted when unrest flared into violence in Oxfordshire, and Somerset had no extra troops to call upon. However, with the likelihood of a rapid end to the trouble in the west Somerset must have felt that the situation was very nearly under control. Then, out of an already troubled sky came news of a major rebellion in East Anglia.

*Which romor soe opened and large in talke of divers persons ascembled att
a certain nyht and daie playe in the towne of Hymondham callyd Wyndham
game which was there played the Satterday nyght being the VI day of June
1549 and held on the VIIth daie and part of the VIIIth daie being Monday,
which daie the people did depart, and they of Wyndham had some conference
to common with such as had not cast downe the same; among whome moving
the same to one Robert Kett alias Knight....*
Nicholas Sotherton - A Commoyson in Norfolk

The East Anglian rebellion of 1549, known today as Kett's rebellion, started in
a simple and, for the period, typical way. On the evening of Saturday the 6th of
July the locals gathered in the pleasant Norfolk market town of Wymondham to
celebrate the feast of the translation of St Thomas a Becket that fell on the
following day. The towns great church, formerly part of the recently dissolved
abbey, was partially dedicated to St Thomas and by tradition his feast was marked
by the performance of plays and general festivities. However, that year the
commoners long pent up grievances, no doubt mixed with large quantities of ale,
turned the celebrations sour and the traditional merriment into rebellious
mayhem.

The previous decade had been a harsh one for the people of East Anglia. The
unprecedented drought of 1542, when the Thames had dried up to a trickle and
salt water reached as far as London bridge, had caused widespread crop failure
and forced many smaller farmers out of business. The following year had been
little better. A fire at Reepham in Norfolk consumed one of the churches and most
of the high street as the river was almost dry and no water was available to
extinguish it, and throughout the region starvation became a very real threat. The
shortage of general foodstuffs, coupled with inflation and a debasement of the
coinage, made the following years both difficult and worrying. With the
commoners in dire need of assistance the perceived wealth of the gentry fostered
resentment and illwill among the lower classes and left them with no option other
than to turn on the upper classes, or turn to the church.

For the townspeople of Wymondham the church of St Thomas had been the
bone of much contention ever since the dissolution of the abbey. At the time of
the abbey's sale the town had negotiated to be allowed to use the priory church, as

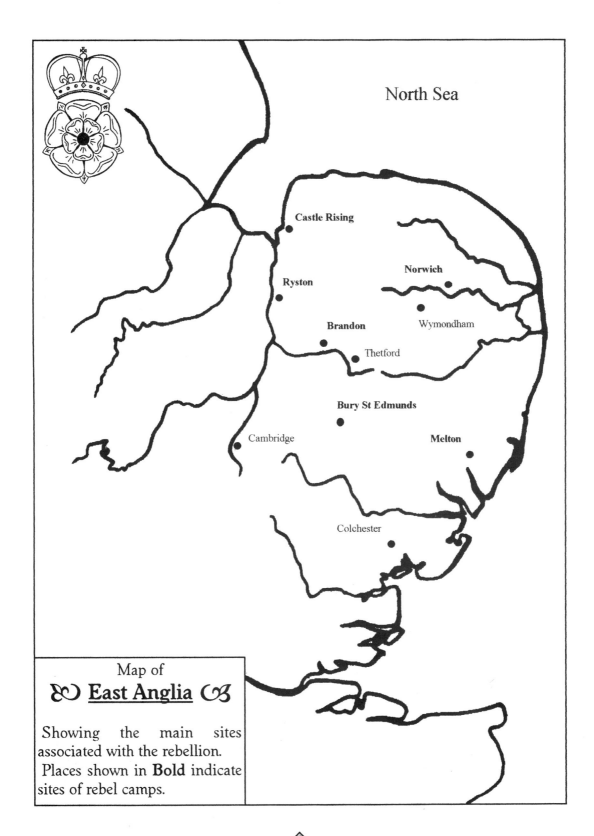

North Sea

Castle Rising

Norwich

Ryston

Brandon

Wymondham

Thetford

Bury St Edmunds

Cambridge

Melton

Colchester

Map of
‘ <u>East Anglia</u> ’

Showing the main sites associated with the rebellion. Places shown in **Bold** indicate sites of rebel camps.

they had always done, as their own parish church. In fact, disputes over its use as a parish church stretched right back to the thirteenth century and the actual rights that the town possessed always appeared unclear. However, upon the dissolution their appeal was granted and while the priory church remained the town's property, the rest of the buildings were to be pulled down under the direction of one John Flowerdew, a local lawyer from nearby Stanfield hall. The town, in their petition to King Henry, had also asked to retain the rights to any other areas of the buildings that shared common fabric with the parish church. Although this was also granted it appears to have been either ignored or misunderstood by the overly efficient Flowerdew.

The townspeople, seeing Flowerdew removing areas of the abbey that they believed they had already paid the King for, grew angry and a heated dispute arose in which Robert Kett, a leading town resident, took a prominent part. Although this dispute seems to have eventually been settled, the townsfolk still felt great resentment towards Flowerdew and he in turn resented Robert Kett. Nearly a decade after the original confrontation both Kett and Flowerdew seem to have been only too happy to continue their quarrel.

The feast of the translation of St Thomas à Becket had always been, for the townsfolk of Wymondham, an opportunity to gather together with their neighbours, gossip, swap news and generally enjoy themselves. However, in 1549 many of those people present seem to have taken the celebrations as an opportunity to discuss and debate the changes that had been recently taking place around them. As a market town that relied upon the surrounding agricultural land for its very existence the subject of local enclosures of common land was obviously going to be a matter of heated contention.

Added to this was the introduction of the new prayer book which, among its many changes, had completely removed all references to St Thomas à Becket from its calendar of festivals. With not only the parish church partially dedicated to the saint but a separate chapel of St Thomas located within the town the locals must have felt that they were being threatened on all sides. Finally after three days of merriment, drinking and argument the townsfolk, no doubt feeling that enough was enough, banded together and turned their hotly spoken words into deeds.

On the evening of Monday July the 8th a group of townspeople marched some three miles to the southwest and tore down the enclosure fences of a Mr Hobart of Morley. Returning via the town and in truculent high spirits the townsfolk then marched a further six miles in the opposite direction towards Hethersett intent on tearing down the fences of the unpopular John Flowerdew. Flowerdew's actions at the time of the dissolution had obviously not been forgotten.

Flowerdew, from what little is known of him today, was obviously a very competent individual. A lawyer of some standing, he held the position of Sergeant at Law, his fortunes were on the increase and he was generally accepted among the ranks of the lesser gentry. His success and profit acquired as King's agent during the disposal of confiscated church property had obviously made him unpopular locally and this was further aggravated by his holding of the Royal post of 'escheator' for the county of Norfolk in the preceding year. The 'escheator' was a crown official who was responsible for any lands within the county that, for any reason, had become forfeit to the King. With dramatic and sweeping powers the post was both profitable and highly unpopular amongst the smaller landowners who, with little or no notice, could be evicted from their holdings.

It appears that Flowerdew, perhaps expecting trouble, learned of the mobs approach before they actually reached his newly enclosed land and intercepted them on the road. Meeting the mob with kind words, and probably a few armed retainers at his back, Flowerdew convinced the rioters that they were mistaken in wanting to tear down his fences. Backing his words with a bribe, said to have been forty pence, he convinced the easily swayed group that the real villain of the piece was Robert Kett, who had also enclosed common land, and suggested that they should return to the area of Wymondham and tear down Kett's fences. The rioters, obviously unsure of themselves when faced with a court official and armed with extra money for ale, turned about face and set off to pull down Kett's enclosure fences.

The Kett family were a well established and respected Wymondham family of moderate status. Of the original five brothers by 1549 only two were still living. The eldest, William, was in his mid sixties and although described as a butcher and mercer in the contemporary accounts appears to have been relatively wealthy and held considerable farming interests in the area. William's sole surviving brother, Robert, was some fifty seven years old at the time the troubles began and was married with five children. Although like his brother primarily a gentleman farmer he appears to have had considerable commercial interests within the town itself and is even described as being a tanner. Although the family's status was played down in the years immediately following the revolt evidence suggests that they had been landowners and merchants in the area since at least the reign of King John and the derisive use of the word 'tanner' probably means that Robert, rather than carrying on the trade himself, actually owned the local rights to it.

How and when Robert Kett heard of the mobs attempt to throw down his fences is unclear, however, as soon as he was aware of the disturbance he rushed to the scene. Following the example set by Flowerdew, Kett confronted the rioters and demanded to know what was going on. The rioters, most of whom it can be assumed knew Kett reasonably well, appear to have then poured forth their grievances and, appealing to Kett's better nature, set forth their views of the injustices that were taking place. Knowing Robert Kett to be a pillar of the local community and staunch supporter of the church they probably hoped for, at the most, his understanding of what they were doing if not his sympathy. What happened next was unusual, if not to say unprecedented.

Kett, after listening to the case put forward by the rioters, actually took a hand in helping them tear down his own fences. The rioters, no doubt gleeful at the ease with which they had converted Kett to their cause, fell on with a vengeance and, their work completed, they were only too happy to follow Kett's lead when he suggested that they should now return to Hethersett and pull down the fences of John Flowerdew. With Kett now nominally at their head the rioters returned to Flowerdew's land and finished the task they had begun earlier that day.

The reasons behind Kett's actions that day have been long debated and interpreted in many different ways by dozens of historians throughout history. Some have suggested that, as a good and devout christian, Kett saw the error of his ways and, in a 'road to Damascus' like conversion, threw in his lot with the oppressed commoners. However, it is also just as likely that Kett, realising that he was going to lose his fences whatever he did, determined to revenge himself on Flowerdew for sending the rioters to his land. By throwing down his own fences and then coercing the rioters into returning to Hethersett, Kett was assuring himself that upon this attempt no amount of money would save Flowerdew's fences.

Although both these arguments probably contain elements of truth it is likely that Kett's real motives fell somewhere between the two. His long standing feud with Flowerdew, begun over the affair of the parish church, no doubt influenced his choice in the next victim of the rioters but, as a local farmer and merchant, he was probably just as concerned about many of the changes taking place as were his neighbours. No doubt the destruction of the enclosures at Hethersett certainly gave him a degree of personal satisfaction but, when it was agreed that the rioters would assemble next day, it was Robert Kett who put himself at their head.

The next morning, Tuesday July the 9th, the rioters once more assembled to discuss what their next move should be. As a popular movement with grievances that they felt were both justifiable and in need of addressing, the rioters decided upon a march on the city of Norwich. As the centre of both the county administration and of regional and national importance the city, with its lawyers and crown officials was the obvious target. Whether the march was actually suggested by Robert Kett remains a mystery but as the ever increasing number of rioters set out to march the few short miles to the city it was Kett who found himself at their head.

The intentions of the rioters in their march upon the city of Norwich is unclear. It is likely that the move was at first only an attempt to gain attention to their plight and to impress upon the local authorities the strength of their feelings. However, as they travelled the nine short miles from Wymondham to Norwich their real intentions became unimportant, as it was their intentions as perceived by the city authorities that really mattered. In fact the local authorities were so alarmed by the approach of this ever increasing body of semi-armed men that, thinking it to be a general rebellion rather than a protest march, they sent immediate messages for aid from both the local gentry and the Royal council that very afternoon.

By evening the rebels, as they were now known, had marched to within two miles of the city walls. With their numbers greatly swelled by protesters joining the march en route, Kett and his followers left the direct road and began to circle to the north of the city. Having perhaps received intelligence concerning the city's state of defensive readiness Kett may have believed the move to the north would gain him time to gather more support.

It is also possible that Kett, who must have known the city very well indeed, realised that if the situation deteriorated into a general fight his poorly armed men would have little hope of attacking the stout walls that defended the city's western approach. By moving his men to the north he could skirt the city and place his rebels to the east where it was protected by nothing but the sluggishly flowing summer river.

As evening fell on the first real day of what can be regarded as the East Anglian rebellion the rebels established the first of their camps at Bowthorpe, about two miles north west of the city walls. Here, continuing the trend set at Wymondham, they pulled down the fences that enclosed an area known as the 'town close'. The close was an area of the countryside that had been enclosed by the city and was, in effect, the city's common land. For a small weekly fee any citizen had the right to graze his animals on the land under the watchful eye of a city employed herdsman. Increased fees and fences had aroused much local hostility and the pulling down of the fences was such a popular move that the rebels were aided by many of the poorer townsfolk of Norwich.

That evening, as the rebels established their camp and Kett began to take stock of the situation, the first of several visitors arrived in their midst. It is believed that the first gentleman to make his appearance was Sir Edmund Wyndham, High Sheriff of both Norfolk and Suffolk. Wyndham, related by marriage to Lord Protector Somerset, had been alerted by the disturbances at Wymondham and had set out to end the uprising before it could gather any momentum. In the absence of the Lord Lieutenant, the Marquis of Northampton who was out of the county, Wyndham was the highest ranking crown official in the area and the quelling of any disturbances fell to him.

Upon arriving at the camp with a small following Wyndham proclaimed them to be in breach of the King's peace and ordered them to disperse and return to their homes. The high handed attitude of the Sheriff and his barely veiled threats seem to have done little but anger the rebels still further and under the threat of violence he was forced to beat a hasty and ignominious retreat into the city.

The next group to visit the rebels camp came from Norwich itself. Thomas Codd, the elected mayor of the city, accompanied by several of the more prominent citizens entered the camp sometime during the evening. Codd, a well spoken of and a kind and generous man, attempted to persuade the rebels to disperse and return to their homes. Obviously of a more diplomatic nature than the Sheriff, Codd was received with courtesy and his request was listened to politely before being turned down by the rebels. Disheartened by his lack of success, but still convinced that bloodshed could be avoided, Codd and his companions rode back to Norwich through the late summer evening.

The next morning, Wednesday the 10th of June, the rebels abandoned their camp at Bowthorpe and, travelling a mile or so to the south, camped in the area of Eaton woods. Relations with the city at this time were still on a relatively amicable footing and Kett probably hoped that rather than having to travel around the north of the city, and cross the river Wensum in the process, that he and his men would be allowed to pass through the city to reach the heath at Mousehold. However, Thomas Codd and the city council, although still wishing to remain on reasonable terms with the rebels, refused permission for them to enter Norwich as they, probably quite rightly, feared that it could lead to their being accused of collaborating with the rebels. It is also likely that, with unrest so widespread throughout the country, they feared that the rebels entry into the city could lead to the disturbances spreading to the city itself.

With their permission to enter the city refused the rebels once more resumed their march around the cities northern perimeter. On the evening of Thursday the 11th the rebel force, now probably numbering well over a thousand men, encamped for the night at Drayton. That evening, as the rebels prepared their evening meals and settled themselves down for the night they had with them the first of what was going to be a large collection of gentlemen prisoners.

Earlier in the day, as the rebels column had reached the Hellesden area, they had been met by the august presence of Sir Roger Wodehouse. Sir Roger, of Kimberley near Wymondham, obviously hoping to use his local knowledge of the Kett family to his advantage, once more attempted to convince the rebels to disperse. Accompanying Wodehouse were several servants and three carts laden with beer and food with which he hoped to be able to bribe the crowd. However, Wodehouse completely misjudged the situation and the rebels, after relieving him of the wagons and their contents, attempted to make him captive. Sir Roger, outraged by the rebels actions, attempted to fight them off but with little success. The struggle ended when Sir Roger, by now stripped of most of his fine clothing and much of his dignity, was driven into a muddy ditch. Still fuming against his mistreatment and railing loudly against the rebels he was only saved from serious physical injury by the quick actions of his servant Edgerley.

The following day, Friday the 12th of June, Kett led the ever expanding rebel band around the northern edge of the city before coming to the edge of Mousehold heath. The heath lay to the east of the city and although not a great height it did give commanding views of activities within the city itself. Honeycombed with chalk and flint mines the majority of the land had been left to pasture with the exception of a few great houses built on the heights out of the smoke and stink of the city. It was one of these great buildings, Surrey House, that Kett finally halted at and requisitioned as his new headquarters.

Surrey House, formerly known as St Leonards Priory, had belonged, since the dissolution, to the family of the Duke of Norfolk. The Dukes son, the Earl of Surrey, had had the site extensively rebuilt and remodelled to serve as his Norfolk home and the site had become known as Surrey House or Mount Surrey. The imprisonment of Norfolk and his son Surrey in the final months of the old King's reign had led to the site being confiscated for the Crown and at the time of Ketts seizure of the house it seems to have been in a poor state of repair. It is interesting to note that as confiscated Crown property the building had been officially under the stewardship of John Flowerdew in his role as 'escheator' for the county of Norfolk. Perhaps, once again, the Kett family feud against John Flowerdew can be said to have influenced the official policy of the rebels. It was from Mount Surrey, even after the occupation of the city itself, that Robert Kett and his fellow leaders oversaw the rebel activities and it was this site that acted as a focus and prison to the great camp that began to grow up around its walls.

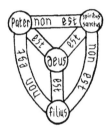

...they first procured a Pryst to minister theyr morninge and evening prayer in the English tounge, then newly begon to bee frequentyd. Also they would have the best men of life and religion to bee their Captains emonge whom they chose one Robert Watson, a preacher of good estimacion, and Thomas Codd, mayor of the Cytte of Norwiche and Thomas Aldrich of Mangrene a two myle from Norwich, a man of good wisdom and honesty and welbelovid; which three persons allthough by no means would be of the conspiracy, yet fearing the aforesaid Robert Kett alias Knight, being wickedly led to be their chief Captain, might by his wicked determinate advise and cowncell procure such great inconveniencies by his preposterous authoritie as ones enterprised and begone might not easily be reverted.

Nicholas Sotherton - The Commoyson in Norfolk

With the establishment of the 'great camp' of rebels on mousehold heath, just to the east of the city of Norwich, the entire nature of Kett's rebellion changed. The disturbance, for at that stage it was really little more, had evolved into something new. Whatever the rebels true intentions on their march from Wymondham to Norwich, traditionally thought to have been no more than a protest to gain the authorities attention, the establishment of a partially armed camp of dissidents outside the defences of the counties capital certainly gave notice that their objectives had changed. The establishment of the camp proved, beyond doubt, that the rebels were there to stay. Come what may, with new recruits entering the camp on an almost hourly basis, it was going to take more than kind words and empty promises to send these men home to their hearths.

The camp on the heath expanded rapidly as did the rebellion as a whole. While new recruits poured into the camp around Mount Surrey other camps, spread around the East Anglian countryside, were established at much the same time. In the west of the county a camp was initially established at Castle Rising, a few miles from the port of Kings Lynn, but local difficulties and the rapid response of the local gentry soon made its site untenable. The rebels, far from being quietly subdued and returning to their homes, moved the camp to a different site at Ryston, just outside Downham Market, where they were established by July 15th.

The actual number of rebels camped in the Downham Market area is unknown but their numbers must have been considerable as, later in the rebellion, the camp was large enough to detach a contingent to Brandon, on the Norfolk\Suffolk border, where a small bridgehead was established in north Suffolk. Elsewhere in Suffolk other camps sprang into life during the long summer days and by the middle of July the entire region was covered in a network of rebel establishments.

At Bury St Edmunds a rebel camp was established early in July and this was followed by a larger camp, perhaps mirroring that of Norwich, coming into existence just outside Ipswich by the 14th. This camp, the main camp in Suffolk, appears to have been organised along much the same lines as its Norwich counterpart and at the height of its power dispensed justice, received petitions and offered an alternative local government to the commoners of the county. Later in the month the Ipswich camp was moved to the village of Melton, just outside Woodbridge. Melton had long been established as the administrative centre for the Dean and Chapter of Ely's liberty of St Audrey and the rebels move there may well have been an attempt to associate their rule with that of the ancient traditions of the old liberty and thereby add a thin veneer of respectability to their newly acquired authority.

A second possible reason for the move from Ipswich to Melton is that Ipswich, along with other east coast ports, was at this time in a state of slight decline. The inflation of the previous decade had combined with the numerous foreign wars of the last years of Henry VIII's reign to produce a slump in international trade. With the towns coffers all but empty it is quite likely that a large number of the rebels actually came from within the town itself. Any attempt by the rebels to hold the actual town would have resulted in a complete blockade by Vice Admiral Wodehouse who was patrolling up and down the east coast. This complete end to foreign trade, if continued for more than a few weeks, would have resulted in severe financial hardship within the town and would have worked against the rebels own long term aims. However, a rebel camp outside the town walls would have had a similar effect by blocking the towns connections with the surrounding countryside. In either case the main loser in each scenario would be Ipswich itself and in the face of local economic collapse the rebels moved to Melton.

At Melton the rebel leaders certainly took their role as an alternative local Government very seriously indeed and, in turn, they were accepted as such by many of the people of east Suffolk. The rebellion, for them, was about righting the wrongs done to the common people by the avaricious local gentry and the rebels believed that they were acting not just in their own best interests, although these surely came high on their agenda, but in the interests of the Crown. An Aldeburgh merchant, seeking redress for a trespass done against him by a local gentleman

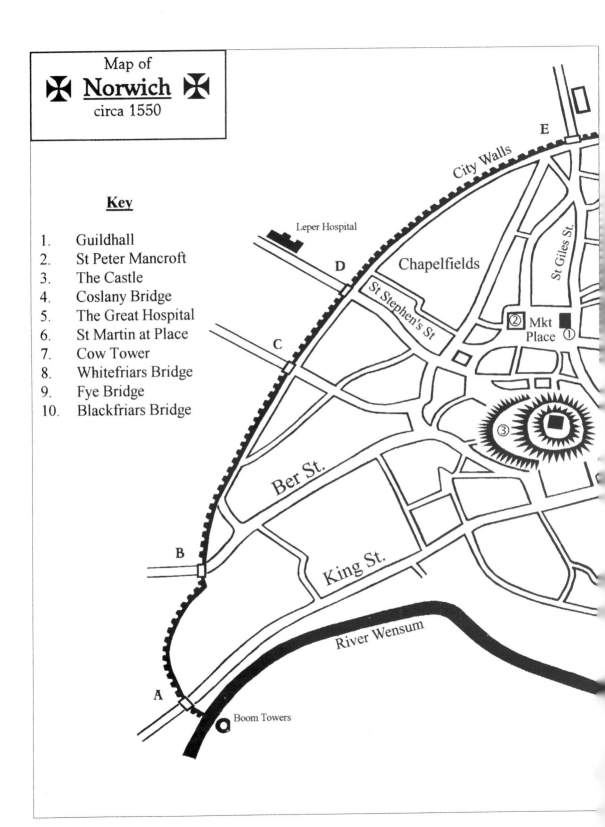

Map of

✠ Norwich ✠

circa 1550

Key

1. Guildhall
2. St Peter Mancroft
3. The Castle
4. Coslany Bridge
5. The Great Hospital
6. St Martin at Place
7. Cow Tower
8. Whitefriars Bridge
9. Fye Bridge
10. Blackfriars Bridge

City Walls

Leper Hospital

D

Chapelfields

St Giles St.

St Stephen's St

② Mkt
Place ①

C

③

Ber St.

B

King St.

A

River Wensum

Boom Towers

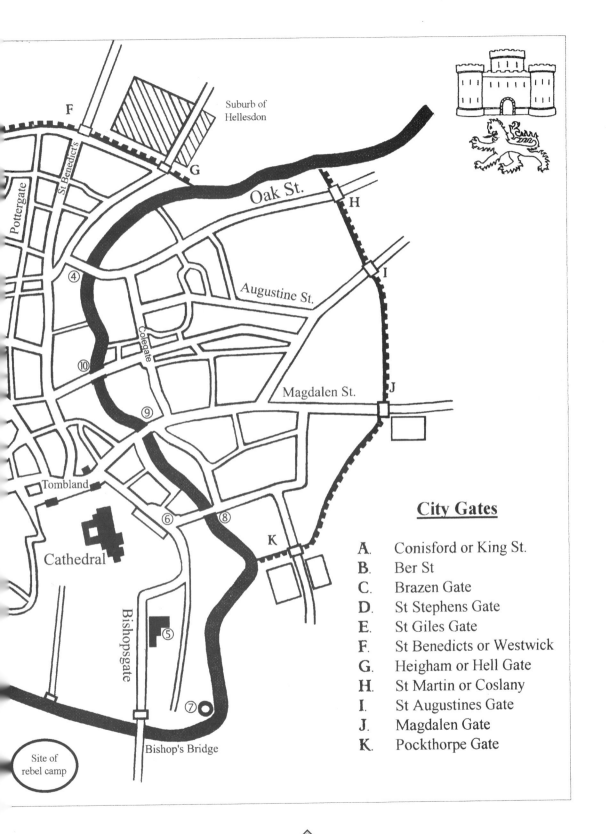

Suburb of
Hellesdon

F

St Benedict's

Pottergate

G

Oak St.

H

④

Augustine St.

I

Colegate

⑩

⑨

Magdalen St.

J

Tombland

⑥   ⑧

K

Cathedral

Bishopsgate

⑤

⑦

Bishop's Bridge

Site of
rebel camp

City Gates

A.	Conisford or King St.
B.	Ber St
C.	Brazen Gate
D.	St Stephens Gate
E.	St Giles Gate
F.	St Benedicts or Westwick
G.	Heigham or Hell Gate
H.	St Martin or Coslany
I.	St Augustines Gate
J.	Magdalen Gate
K.	Pockthorpe Gate

known as Francis Jerny, took his complaint to the rebels at Melton. Here he probably felt that he would gain a fairer hearing than in the local courts where, in all likelihood, the magistrates would not only know of Jerny but be closely associated with him.

These attacks by the rebels against what they perceived to be the self interest of the county gentry continued to be one of the main justifications for the existence of the rebel camps. The commoners felt that over the previous decades both their rights and access to justice had been considerably diminished by the greed and avarice of the gentry and, believing that they were in fact likely to gain at least the sympathy of central government, they wished to redress the balance on a local level. By taking the reins of local government into their own hands they believed they were re-establishing the status quo and supporting the power of the monarch.

At the same time that the camps at Bury, Downham, Melton and Norwich were coming into being there were attempts at both Great Yarmouth and Cambridge to establish similar camps. These early uprisings by the commoners were put down by the local authorities who, for once, acted with both energy and vigour. The fact that a camp was not established at Cambridge can be said to have had a significant effect on the outcome of the rebellion as a whole. A camp at Cambridge would have completed the ring of camps that, in effect, alienated the great camp at Norwich from the rest of the country. If the rebels had gained a foothold in Cambridge then the only way in which government forces could approach Norwich would have been via another camp.

At the great camp on Mousehold heath things were moving on apace. One of the first acts of the rebels was to appoint a priest to oversee the religious observances held in the camp. Nicholas Sotherton in his 'commoyson in Norfolk' specifically points out that the priest was to say the prayers in the English tongue. This early and universal use of the reformed prayer book by the Norfolk rebels is obviously the main factor that separates them from their Cornish contemporaries. Unlike the conservative Cornishmen the East Anglians agreed with the majority of the religious changes and, as can be seen from the list of demands drawn up later, wished for a comparative reform amongst the local clergy.

This radical Protestantism that appears to have been fairly widely spread among the East Anglian population had its roots, much like that of enclosures themselves, in the wool trade. Close contact with the low countries, the Protestant hotbed of Europe, and the importation of Flemish weavers into the region to enhance the cloth trade no doubt had the knock on effect of introducing many of the locals to their ideas of reformed religion. This exposure to radically new religious ideals, coupled with what the commoners perceived as a corruption in the established church led to the region being at the forefront of the Protestant and Puritan movements of the next two centuries.

This left the government in London now dealing with two very different rebellions coupled with a small series of nationwide disturbances. The disturbances focused their discontent on both religious reform and enclosure while the Cornish rebellion, in an area where enclosure was having little impact, focused almost solely on religion. This then left them with a major rebellion in East Anglia where religious issues were sidelined and land reforms were of paramount importance. The Protector's confused and inefficient response to the situation suddenly, when viewed as a whole, not only becomes understandable but appears almost excusable.

The camp at Mousehold began to organise itself into a serious rival to the local authorities in Norwich. A collection of leaders, all under the overall supervision of Robert Kett, was appointed to oversee the policies of the rebels and the general day to day running of the camp's affairs. The fact that the Norwich authorities were still, at this stage, unsure of how to react to the presence of the rebel camp is shown in the appointment of the rebel's spokesmen. Both Thomas Codd, the mayor, and Thomas Aldrich, a prominent citizen, were co-opted onto the council to serve under Kett and throughout the peaceful weeks in the immediate aftermath of the rebel's advance appear to have spent as much of their time on the heath as they did in the city.

Thomas Aldrich, like Codd was a well known and well respected local gentleman. Born locally to parents of relatively modest means Thomas rose to become one of the wealthiest men in the county. He had first served as Sheriff of Norwich as far back as 1497 and had twice been elected as the city's Mayor. A competent business man he had become not just a great landowner, holding acres between Norwich and Wymondham, but also a rich merchant. In the assessment of 1525 Thomas Aldrich was found to the second richest man in Norwich. Aldrich appears to have commanded the respect of both sides during the rebellion and been fairly active throughout the difficulties, no mean feat for a man who was apparently already well over seventy years of age.

Alongside both Codd and Aldrich was chosen a third person from the city to advise Kett and stand up for the city's rights. Robert Watson a 'preacher in those days of good estimacion', according to Sotherton, was co-opted along side the other two and together the three of them appear to have been given preference over the rest of the rebel council. This advancement of their positions among the rebel advisers may be a symbol of the high regard in which they were held but is more likely an indication that both Kett and his allies understood the importance of good propaganda. Three prominent city characters siding openly with the rebels would do much to sway the hearts and minds of those wavering in the rebels favour.

The rest of the council, or at least the vast majority of it, appears to have been elected by the men of the camp. Two representatives from each hundred of the county would serve as spokesmen for their fellows in all matters and in all over fifty names of these 'governors' have been recorded. Covering most of Norfolk and even bits of Suffolk, the list indicates exactly how widespread the rebellion had actually become. The 'governors' represented to Kett and his fellow leaders the wishes of the general population of the camp and appear to have been an integral part of the camps quasi-democratic administration.

The first two weeks of the rebels rule at Mousehold were relatively uneventful and generally peaceful. The relations with the city were, if not warm, at least cordial and a certain amount of traffic took place between the two sites. Kett's objective, to prove that the county could be governed effectively and honestly by honest men, seemed to have been almost attained. Parish and town authorities began to cooperate with the rebels, supplies were obtained and commissions issued for the collection of food from the surrounding countryside. In Carlton Coleville the parish officers collected money under the orders of Kett and had it transported to the camp on the heath while John of Great Yarmouth, a local merchant and brewer, was ordered to return home and bring back a barrel of beer for the rebels use.

The rebel numbers were also increasing on a daily basis. From across the region men flocked to the camp to join the rebel's fight for justice. These men however, were not all dispossessed commoners and disgruntled individuals as many of the accounts would have us believe. Among their number were official delegations from many of the local parishes sent to represent their fellow parishioners interests.

From North Elmham, a parish ten miles to the west of the city, arrived a contingent led by the parish constable and funded by the parish authorities. Undoubtedly not unique this contingent represents the extent to which the rebel authorities were becoming accepted as an alternative form of local government. In all it appeared that the countryside was as willing to accept the rule of Kett and his well meaning rebels as they were to follow the orders issued by the King's officers.

For Robert Kett and his fellow rebels the short period after the establishment of the camp at Mount Surrey must have seemed like a midsummer dream. They had achieved almost total control of the area with virtually no opposition and little bloodshed. They had begun to establish a fairer form of local government, one based upon justice and not just the word of the law, and their writ was accepted by Royal officers in many areas of the county. They had managed to feed their men, no mean feat in itself, and their commissioners travelled the countryside bearing warrants issued in the King's name. In effect, in those first few weeks after the march to Norwich, it would have been difficult to visualize how things could have gone better.

The rule established by Kett upon the heath was one of overall fairness. He aimed not to overthrow the government but rather have it re-establish the good rights of the common people. With this in mind the rebels upon the heath established their own form of debating chamber. Laying planks across the stout boughs of an oak tree a form of platform was built. It was here at the 'Tree of the Reformation' that Kett and his fellow leaders addressed their men and in turn heard the cases of supposed injustice that were brought before them.

The reaction of the citizens of Norwich to the initial establishment of the rebels camp that sat overlooking their fine city was cautious. Although the rebels found many supporters amongst the poorer classes of townsfolk the more wealthy citizens were, of course, wary of an armed body of commoners who held a large grudge against the well off. However, with no military support and heavily outnumbered even within the walls of the city itself the gentry, along with virtually everybody else, had no choice but to comply with the rebels demands. The city fathers, perhaps attempting to justify their inaction against Kett's forces, even went as far as pointing out that for them to raise a military force without Royal consent, even if it was designed to subdue rebellion, was a treasonous act in itself.

In the beginning the demands placed by the rebels upon the city and its inhabitants were very simple. The camp, now swollen to many thousands in number, wanted access to the markets, and provisions of the city and its merchants. Although not allowing the rebels to enter en masse the city authorities appear to have complied with these early demands and, under the watchful gaze of Kett, Codd and Aldrich, a form of mutual cooperation became the daily norm. Codd and Aldrich appear to have been acting in what they perceived to be the city's best interests. By cooperating with Kett they gave the rebels no excuse to vent their anger upon the city and perhaps saved many lives. However, the close association of Codd and Aldrich with Kett was to later lead them into charges of having collaborated with the enemy.

Although collaboration is obviously too strong a word to use when referring to the actions of Codd and Aldrich it is easy to understand why government officials could have judged it so. All the commissions issued by the rebels for the collection of provisions from the surrounding areas were countersigned by Kett, Codd and Aldrich and the list of rebel demands, sent to the council in London and drawn up at the camp on Mousehold, also bore the three signatures. To an ill informed outsider it could all too easily appear that Codd and Aldrich, rather than acting under the threatening orders of the rebels, had thrown in their lot with Robert Kett.

It was during these first few 'honeymoon' weeks of the rebellion that the actual political objectives of the rebels were more clearly defined. Kett, no doubt advised by his 'governors' and sympathetic priests, compiled a list of demands that the rebels wished to be fulfilled by the Government in London. The twenty nine demands make interesting reading and give a very clear indication of the rebels, rather modest, aims (See Appendix 1). Based almost entirely on the idea of righting the wrongs done to the commoners over the previous decades, the list of demands clearly indicates the economic background to the events of the summer of 1549. In fact, the religious element is limited to less than ten of the demands, and even these deal mainly with the financial dealings of the clergy rather than any points of doctrine.

The Council of State's response to the rebel demands was predictable. On the 21st of July a Herald arrived from London and offered the rebels a full pardon for their 'crimes' if they would disperse and return to their homes. The issues brought up in the list of twenty nine demands were not even touched upon. Now, stung into action by the government's response to the rebels, the authorities within the city of Norwich took action. Realising that now the central government had made the position of the rebels clear, that they could no longer allow themselves to co-operate on even a superficial basis, the city leaders severed all ties with the camp.

The Aldermen and gentlemen of Norwich now determined to make a stand. Without the markets and warehouses of the city they believed that the camp would soon be forced to disperse due to lack of supplies. With the city gates tightly shut and the militia guarding them, the walls manned and the half dozen city cannon put in place to cover any rebel attack, Norwich prepared to fight.

The rebels on the heath now knew that the situation had come to a head. They had been disappointed by the Heralds reply to their demands but had no intention of dispersing so easily. They had come to prove that they were the ones standing up for justice and were determined to carry on with their protest. However, with Norwich now lying hostile below them, its markets denied them and its citizens armed against them, the rebels knew they were in a precarious position. They needed Norwich to be able to survive. Not just its markets and food supplies but its prestige. Without the county capital and its administration under their command any pretence at being the rightful local government would be useless. Without the support of the city the camps life would be very limited indeed. They had no choices left to them.

On the evening of July 21st 1549, the day of the rebels rejection of the Heralds offer, Kett's army encamped upon Mousehold heath and around Mount Surrey attacked the city of Norwich. With cannon captured and taken from, among other places Paston Hall, the rebel artillery opened fire on their fellow countrymen. Flashes filled the night sky and ball after ball crashed into the city below the rebel guns. After a little over two weeks, the uprising led by Robert Kett to re-establish the rights of the commoners had transformed itself into bloody and open rebellion.

A fine old city, truly, is that, view it from what side you will; but it shows best from the east, where the ground, bold and elevated, overlooks the fair and fertile valley in which it stands.... Yes, there it spreads from north to south, with its venerable houses, its numerous gardens, its thrice twelve churches, its mighty mound.... There is a grey old castle upon the top of that mighty mound; and yonder rising three hundred feet above the soil, from among those noble forest trees, behold that Norman masterwork, that cloud encircled cathedral spire...

George Borrow 1803 - 1881

In that hot summer of 1549 the physical defences of the city of Norwich left much to be desired. Years of neglect combined with rapid growth, caused by the wealth that flowed through the city gates from the cloth trade, had left the defences in a state of decay that offered little real protection to the borough. A professional Tudor soldier, well versed in the arts of gunnery and siege craft, would have had little trouble capturing the town. However, Kett's men included few professionals and even after years of poor maintenance the city defences would still give pause for thought to the ill equipped commoners that made up the majority of Kett's army.

In 1549 the city of Norwich was, in effect, split into two very distinct areas. The majority of the city sat to the south nestled in a wide loop created by the river Wensum. The remaining area, about a third of the cities acreage lay to the north of the river and was bounded to the west and south by the river. This area, known as 'Norwich over the water' or simply 'Norwich over', was linked to the main town via four bridges and although probably the site of the earliest settlement appears to have been very much the poorer end of town. With the Cathedral, castle and most of the principle buildings in the southern section 'Norwich over' was little more than an extensive and ancient suburb.

It appears to have been this area, along Magdalen street and its surrounding alleys, that suffered a devastating fire in 1507. The fire is reputed to have burnt for four days and nights before finally being brought under control and extinguished. The area of the fire remained desolate for years afterwards as many former inhabitants seem to have preferred to rebuild elsewhere and in 1534 the city council tried to order the inhabitants to either rebuild their dwellings or, at the very least, wall in the ruins so that they would not pose a menace to the other people of Norwich.

For its defence Norwich had relied, throughout the troubled medieval period on three individual items. The first, the castle, had been originally built shortly after the Norman conquest and was of the motte and bailey variety. Built as a Royal fortress the castle was designed to subdue the inhabitants of the city rather than defend them and its initial construction had involved the demolition of many dozens of the original city buildings. The keep, built of Caen stone and one of the most massive of its type, sat atop the motte and underwent few obvious changes throughout its long history. The surrounding bailey had been altered and extended many times, but by the Tudor period its earthworks were in a poor state of repair and its walls were crumbling.

Situated as it was in the very heart of the city the castle could play little part in the defence of the perimeter and as such it had long before been relegated to little more than an administrative centre and county prison. The keep, if adequately defended, could perhaps be used as a final refuge but other than that appeared to be of little practical use in the fight against the rebels.

The second of the city's defences were its walls. The city council, who were responsible for the upkeep and maintenance of the walls, first gained permission for their construction in 1294 and they were again extensively improved and repaired in the early fourteenth century. The walls stretched for over two miles and were pierced by a dozen large gates which were, in turn, protected by a variety of gate-houses. The most notable of these gate-houses were St Stephens gate, which covered the London road; Ber Street gate, which led to the castle; St Benedicts (or Westwick); and a separate gate-house that covered the river crossing at Bishopsgate.

The northern side of the city was served by four gates the principal of which was the Magdalen gate and it was here that the common gallows were situated. The city walls ended just to the east of this area and combined with the river made the whole of 'Norwich over', as it was sometimes known, a self contained area within the city walls.

Although they were no doubt in less than perfect condition by the time of Kett's rebellion the city council had made continuous efforts to keep the walls in relatively good order and the city records are full of accounts of money being spent on their repair. The actual line of the wall was over twenty feet high and, in places, nearly eight feet thick and supported a series of circular and semi-circular bastions or towers that stood proud of the walls face.

The obvious main drawback to the city walls, apart from their expense which the townsfolk were forever complaining about, was the fact that they did not run the full length of the city's perimeter. A short stretch to the west, where the river cut back to the north around 'Norwich over', had no wall and the entire eastern side of the main city's edge relied upon nothing but the river Wensum for its protection. In effect the Wensum was the cities third defence but in a hot summer, as it was in 1549, the water level would have been dangerously low. This eastern perimeter, the area that faced Mousehold heath and the rebel camp, had only one point of crossing, at Bishops bridge, and although protected by a large gate-house, would have been extremely vulnerable to attack.

At the southern extremity of the unprotected eastern edge of the city's boundary lay the 'Devils tower'. This tower actually lay on the further side of the river, outside the city perimeter, and formed one half of the boom towers that protected the river approach to the city. The boom, consisted of two chains of 'Spanish iron' that were slung across the river, was probably more used as a customs control than an actual defence and with a tower on each bank it could just as easily be used by the rebels to stop river traffic as it could by the city.

To the north of Bishops Bridge, protecting the northern flank of the city where the river turned west, stood the 'Cow Tower'. This large detached bastion is first recorded as being present in the fourteenth century and probably acquired its name from its position, sited as it was in the old cow pasture (cowholme) of the Cathedral. By the time of the rebellion the tower was probably acting as some form of detached artillery bastion that helped to cover the city's river approach. Although an impressive structure the tower would have been of only limited use during the siege as it was designed with an earlier form of warfare in mind and its brick and infill construction would have had trouble withstanding a concerted artillery bombardment. Although a deterrent to lightly armed troops attempting to cross the river, the Cow Tower became virtually useless as soon as a bridgehead was established on the western bank, as all its embrasures but one faced away from the city.

From the rebels perspective, looking down upon the city from the east, the defences must have seemed very flimsy indeed. From their vantage point at Mount Surrey they would have had a clear view of the whole eastern perimeter of the city.

To their left they would have been able to make out the distant bulk of the boom towers while to their right they would have plainly seen the impressive Cow tower standing guard at the bend in the river. Before them, spread like a map upon the landscape, lay the bulk of the city separated from them by the sluggishly flowing river Wensum. Directly before and below them lay the river crossing.

Bishops bridge, guarded by the small keep like gate-house, was their entrance to the city. Once across the bridge the rebels would be free to march towards the Cathedral down the lightly built up Bishopsgate street or spread out to north and south across the water meadows that still lay unencumbered by houses along the bank of the river. Only at the far southern end of the city did the wharfs, warehouses and dwellings actually reach as far as the riverside.

And to make all sure in the nyght the ordenaunce of the cytie was placed alongst the ryver with good guard of men in the Hospitall Myddowes for that it was the weakest place, and as they of the Cytie shott att them, they did the like into the cyttie all nyght and the rebellis percieving in the morninge that theyr shot went over the Cyttye they browte downe theyr Ordenaunce from the lower part of the hyll, but fearing to remaine there for that the cyttie shot drive them off whereuppon theyr Ordenaunce did small hurt.
Nicholas Sotherton - The Commoyson in Norfolk

That Sunday night, the 21st day of July, the sound of cannon fire shattered the peaceful sleep of the citizens of Norwich. The Mayor and council had had little choice but to shut the gates against the rebels after their refusal to heed the words of the Royal Herald and prepare to defend themselves. Inaction on their part would be looked upon as collaboration but, as the Herald had brought no military support to the beleaguered city, it seemed all too likely that the city's defensive preparations would be in vain. Faced as they were by many thousands of rebels, who could probably count on the support of scores of citizens within the city itself, and with little in the way of armament, the city would be hard pressed to beat off even the lightest of attacks.

The first actions of the council was to establish its own gun positions to be able to bombard, and perhaps dishearten, the rebel camp. The majority of the city ordinance, along with two larger cannon sent by Sir William Paston from his home at Caister castle, were installed on the castle ditches. Being one of the highest points in the city the cannon could fire over the houses and river to reach the heath. While these guns were being positioned a smaller fieldpiece was manoeuvred into the common staitheyard where, commanded by the two Appleyard brothers who had until that evening been Ketts prisoners, it covered the river. The obvious deficiencies of the defences at Bishops bridge were also recognised and a hasty attempt was made to throw up earthworks to either side of the gate-house.

Once the guns on castle ditches were in position and with darkness falling as the late summer evening drew in, the city's guns opened fire. The shots from the city were soon answered by the rebel artillery entrenched upon the heath. As darkness closed around the beleaguered city, bright flashes showed where the castle guns and the rebel guns duelled through the night.

At first light the gunfire appears to have ceased. Neither the city's bombardment of the camp on Mousehold heath or the rebels reply seems to have been very effective and little damage was recorded. The rebels, taking advantage of the temporary ceasefire, took the opportunity to move their guns down off the heath. They had probably had trouble depressing their gun barrels far enough to effectively target the city defences, and by moving their firing position could more easily bring their fire to bear on the gates at Bishops bridge. However, during the same lull the city defenders had also taken the opportunity to reposition their pieces. They had now established six guns in the meadows behind the 'hospitall' in Bishopsgate street, a bare hundred yards behind the earthworks at Bishops bridge and no more than a quarter of a mile from the rebel's new gun position.

Now as the sun rose on the morning of Monday, the 22nd of July, the rebel guns once again began to fire upon the city from their new positions. However, as soon as the city ordinance returned fire the rebel guns found themselves under severe pressure. A short range artillery duel was bound to end in the crippling of at least one sides gun batteries, if not both and the rebels, fearing to lose their cannon before they had entered the city, withdrew once more to the safety of the heath.

At this point Robert Kett drew a temporary halt to the escalating violence. Perhaps in an attempt to prevent further bloodshed Kett sent two envoys, James Williams a tailor and Ralph Sutton a hatter, both of Norwich, under a flag of truce to talk to the Mayor. Kett's message was simple; either the city council gave the rebels right of passage into the city to collect supplies or else the rebels would storm the city and take what they wanted. Perhaps Kett naively believed that under such pressure the council would back down, however, with the words of the Royal Herald still ringing in their ears the council had no option but to refuse Kett's offer. As the flag of truce was lowered and the messengers returned to the camp on the heath the rebel guns once more opened fire.

As the first of the rebel cannon balls once more descended upon the city, the half dozen guns in the hospital meadow began to return fire. Now firing uphill they had little chance of success, but with the rebel guns once again high on the heath they were also relatively safe from the rebel shots. After a short and apparently ineffective artillery duel Kett decided that his only option lay in a general assault on the Bishops bridge and the gate-house at its western end. Leading his massive force down from the heights of Mousehold heath Kett's rebels were met by a storm of arrows from the archers stationed in the gate-house and the newly erected earthworks around it. However, the archers seem to have had little enthusiasm for the task as Sotherton recounts '*so impudent were they (the rebels) and soe desperate that of theyr vagabond boyes..... came emong the thickett of the arrows and gathered them up when some of the seid arrows stack fast in theyr leggs and other parts and did therwith most shamefully turn up theyr bare tayles agenst those which did shoote, whych soe dysmayed the Archers that it tooke theyr hart from them.*'

The city archers, for some reason disheartened by the sight of the rebels bare backsides, caused few casualties. The rebels took to the river and at about midday crossed the Wensum armed with '*halbers, spers, swerds and other weapons, and some with muck forks, pytch forks etc*'. The city gunners now faced with a massive force on their side of the river, and running low on powder, fled back into the maze of city streets leaving their guns to fall into the rebels hands. Bishops bridge and the stout gate-house found itself suddenly outflanked and desparately outnumbered. The defenders, following the gunners lead, abandoned their defences and fled into the city. In a matter of a single morning, and with few casualties, the rebels had captured the city.

The rebels, having now secured their entry into the city, swarmed through the narrow streets to occupy the whole city centre. Congregating at the market place, beneath the fine old market cross, the rebels were faced once more with the Royal Herald who had addressed them only the previous afternoon on the heath. The Herald, perhaps realising that he was in part responsible for the latest turn of events, attempted to disperse the rebels by once more reading the Royal proclamation aloud. The rebels, now in jubilant mood after their easy victory, jeered and shouted him down. In fear of his life the Herald, aided by the deputy Mayor Augustine Steward, fled the city and set out back to London.

With the city in rebel hands, Kett's next move was to strip it of its means of defence. Probably realising that he could not allow his forces to remain at large within the city walls for fear of general disorder and looting, he returned to his camp on the heath, taking with him the captured city guns and as much powder and shot as he could find. The city's armouries had been emptied and the rebels had even gone as far as forcing the city Chamberlain to assist them in emptying the Guildhall of its stores where they requisitioned powder, bullets and pikes.

Upon his return to his headquarters at Mount Surrey, Kett took with him a large collection of prisoners from the city. These captives included Thomas Codd, the Mayor, Thomas Aldrich and several of the city's more prominent residents and

Braun and Hofenberg's plan map of Norwich 1581. This perspective map of Norwich, one of the earliest known, clearly shows many of the principal sites associated with Kett's rebellion. In the background Mousehold Heath and Mount Surrey, site of the rebel camp, is clearly visible just above the Cathedral. With the city defences clearly marked the map gives a vivid impression of the thriving city that became the scene of so much bloody conflict during the uprising. Copyright - Norfolk Museums Service (Norwich Castle Museum).

Norwich Cathedral looking North. It was here that the Earl of Warwick established an observation post and first noticed the rebel withdrawal towards Dussindale. Augustine Steward's house and the Maids Head Tavern are both situated in Tombland which is shown at the extreme left of the photograph. Along the top of the picture the river Wensum can be seen flowing west to east. The two bridges, Fye Bridge and Whitefriars, are two of the original four bridges that connected central Norwich with 'Norwich over'. Copyright - Derek A. Edwards, Norfolk Museums Service.

Castle Rising. Aerial photograph viewed from the south. It was here, a few miles from Kings Lynn, that the west Norfolk rebels first tried to establish a camp. However, due to strong local opposition the rebels were forced to abandon the site in favour of a new camp at Ryston just outside Downham Market. Copyright - Timescape Publishing.

Norwich Castle 1738. This etching, by Samuel and Nathaniel Buck, clearly shows the massive earthwork thrown up to support the keep. The surrounding earthworks, known as 'castle ditches' mark the position occupied by the city cannon during the first bombardment of the rebel camp on Mousehold Heath. The keep was used as a prison by both the city authorities and the rebels and it was here that Robert Kett and his brother William spent their last days prior to their executions. Copyright - Norfolk Museums Service (Norwich Castle Museum).

Brazen Gates. This small gatehouse defended the entry to the city that lay directly to the south of St. Stephen's. While Warwick's artillery was bombarding St. Stephen's gate, word reached him that the Brazen gates were in poor condition and could easily be forced. Acting upon this advice Warwick sent a detachment of pioneers forward and within a few minutes the gates had been taken. This then led to further heavy fighting taking place in the streets behind the gate. Etching by H. Ninham.

Augustine Steward. Steward was one of the few local citizens to emerge from the rebellion with any credit to his name. As Deputy Mayor of Norwich in 1549 he controlled the city whilst his superior, Mayor Thomas Codd, was held by the rebels. It was Steward, helped by several fellow Aldermen, who managed to open St. Benedict's Gate and allow the Earl of Warwick and his army entry into the beleaguered city. Copyright - Norfolk Museums Service (Norwich Castle Museum).

St. Benedict's Gate. While Warwick's forces were busy engaging the rebels in street fighting around both the Brazen Gates and St. Stephen's Gates Augustine Steward, the cities Deputy Mayor, managed to secure the gates on St. Benedict's and inform Warwick of his action. The Earl quickly marched north to St. Benedict's gates where he entered the city. Advancing towards the market place Warwick manages to capture a group of rebels who were retreating from his other attacks on St. Stephen's Gates and had them hung from the Market Cross. Etching by H. Ninham.

Bishops Gate Bridge. The bridge on Bishops Gate, which still survives to this day, was the scene of most of the heavy fighting during the rebellion. Twice the gatehouse was defended, with earthworks being thrown up on either side, and twice the rebels managed to outflank the defenders and capture the bridge. The gatehouse shown here is the late Tudor replacement erected after the original twin towered structure was badly damaged by the rebels. Under constant bombardment one of the original great towers was sent crashing to the ground killing many of the defenders. Etching by H. Ninham.

The Cow Tower. This massive tower stands on a bend in the river just to the north of Bishops Bridge. Acting as a detached bastion it covered the river approach to the city quay and although well within sight of the rebel attacks it played little part in the city's defence as the majority of its embrasures face away from the scene of the fighting. However, tradition states that the tower was hit by the rebel artillery who damaged its roof. Copyright - Brian Ayers, Norfolk Museums Service.

St. Stephen's Gate. This gateway, one of the twelve that pierced Norwich's stout walls, straddled the main road that led towards Cambridge and London. It was here that the Earl of Warwick first attempted to gain entry to the rebel held city. Establishing his artillery outside the walls he bombarded the gates until they were finally broken in. His trained soldiers quickly exploited the breach and heavy fighting took place in the streets behind the gateway. Etching by H. Ninham.

were probably incarcerated as a guarantee of the goodwill of the city. By removing some, but not all, of the city's governors, Kett probably hoped to ensure the good behaviour of the rest. However, by removing the well meaning Mayor, Kett had inadvertently placed the command of the city in the hands of his more than competent deputy Augustine Steward.

Steward, a wealthy and well respected merchant, had already been Mayor of Norwich twice before and, according to Sotherton, was *'a good and modest man, hee was beloved of poore and rich and att this well contentid of many to bee obeyid.'* His house, a fine timber framed building, still stands in Tombland and it was from here that he conducted operations during the tense few days after the rebel assault. Steward was in the unenviable position of being responsible for keeping order within the city walls while his superior was being held captive, and the streets were full of excited rebel troops. However, he seems to have risen to the occasion and reports of rebel outrages and subsequent unrest within the city are few and far between. In fact, after the troubles, it is Augustine Steward who is singled out for praise for his actions during the rebel occupation of Norwich.

Kett's refusal to disband his force when ordered to by the Herald and his subsequent assault upon the city of Norwich, finally and irrevocably changed the nature of the rebellion. Up until the arrival of the Herald the rebels had expected the understanding, if not outright support, from the government in London. The Herald's message had made it quite clear that neither would be forthcoming and, in the eyes of those who governed England, Kett and his men were no more than traitors. Now, having seized the city, Kett could expect a Royal army to come against him and put down the rebellion within a matter of days.

With time now of the essence, Kett and his men set about completing the tasks they had set for themselves; the reform of local government. In the week that followed the capture of Norwich, Kett and his fellow 'governors', operating from Mount Surrey and the 'tree of reformation', began to instigate a series of hearings and trials of local gentlemen accused of abusing their rights and powers. The Chamberlain of Norwich was confronted by over a hundred rebels who wished to take him to the tree where he would be tried for leading part of the defence of the city against them. However, his pleas of innocence were so oiled with silver that he managed to bribe the mob into allowing him to go free. Others, however, were not so lucky and Sotherton records that:-

'Kett use dayly to call the Gentlemen prisoners before him into the tree of Reformacion which was not done wythout the whole multitude, and them they had noe complaints of

they cryd 'A good man, a good man!' the other that were complaind of they cryid 'Hang him, hang him!' wythout further judgement...'

Rapid and popularist as these 'trials' were Kett appears to have kept a level head during the proceedings and although many of the gentlemen were placed in close confinement none appear to have actually been strung up by the angry mob. In fact Kett seems to have been remarkably lenient with many of his prisoners and within a few days Thomas Codd, after the intercession of the other prisoners, was offered his freedom to return to the city. Codd, however, was more of a political animal than many people have given him credit for and while gratefully accepting his freedom chose to spend most of his time at the camp; leaving the tense atmosphere of the city under the watchful gaze of Augustine Steward.

While all these events were taking place in the city of Norwich and the heath above it, the government in London were not being slow to react. The Herald had no doubt made a hasty ride back to London to report on the actions of the rebels, and Somerset, probably alarmed by the eyewitness report of events taking place so near the capital, hastily put together a force to march on Norwich.

And after xiiii or or xvi daies it pleased the King's Majesty to send downe to Norwich to represse theis Rebellis ye Lord Marquis of Northampton wyth the Lord Sheffeyld, the old Lord Waydsworth and others number of Knights as Sir Anthony Denny, Sir Ralph Sadler, Sir Richard a Lee, Sir Richard Southwell and dyvers other Knights, Squyers and Gentyllmen and dyvers Italians, strangers and others to the number of xii or xiiiC persons...
Nicholas Sotherton - The Commoyson in Norfolk

On the morning of Wednesday, the 31st day of July, the Royal army, under the command of Sir William Parr Marquess of Northampton, finally arrived within sight of the walls of Norwich. That first day the army camped within a mile of the city walls and, thinking Norwich to be entirely in rebel hands, sent forward a Herald to summon the city to surrender. This summons by the Herald was answered by the deputy Mayor, Augustine Steward.

At the approach of the Royal army Kett had once more withdrawn to the heath along with the majority of his troops. The rebels would have had as much trouble holding the city against professional troops as the city authorities had against Kett and the rebels probably thought that by allowing the army to enter the city they were placing them at a disadvantage. Within the narrow streets and alleys Kett's local men would have the advantage and be able to retake the city at will. It must also be presumed that, at this time, Kett wished to avoid an all out fight with an enemy of unknown strength.

In military terms Kett really had very little to fear from Northamptons newly arrived army. Although a competent military leader of proven ability the Marquis had been given few resources with which to quell a rebellion of this size. His troops numbered probably less than 1500 men and of these a large part were Swiss, German and Italian mercenaries who, although highly efficient battlefield troops, had little understanding of the delicate situation in which they now found themselves. The rest of Northampton's force was probably made up of the personal retainers of the many Knights and Esquires who accompanied him and were unlikely to be enthusiastic at the prospect of fighting fellow countrymen.

Upon hearing the Heralds summons Augustine Steward sent a message to the Mayor who, at this time, was still lodged within the camp on the heath. The

Mayor, with the full knowledge of Kett and the council, sent word to Steward that the army was to allowed entry into the city. Steward now hastened to St Stephens gate, which blocked the main road to London, and there presented the Herald with the city's sword of state and explained the absence of the Mayor. The Herald then returned to the main army which, led by a bareheaded Sir Richard Southwell carrying the sword, entered the turbulent streets of Norwich.

Northampton's first act upon entering the city was to attempt to secure the city perimeter and to oust any remaining rebels from within the walls. He firstly travelled to the great market place where, at the Guildhall, he met with the city's remaining councillors and learnt what he could of the local situation. From here, with his men spreading out through the streets, he proceeded to the house of Augustine Steward in Tombland where he and his followers are said by Sotherton to have *'rested in they're armore uppon cushions and pillows'*.

With Northampton now established at Steward's house his troops set to guarding the city. Towards evening a few skirmishes with small scouting parties of rebels took place and the streets came alive to the sounds of sporadic gunfire. In most cases the rebels were easily pushed back but in one incident an Italian, by the name of Cheavers, was captured by an advance party of rebels who carried off the unfortunate soldier to the camp on the heath. There on the heath, with feelings against the mercenaries running high, the unfortunate Cheavers was hung from the walls of Mount Surrey. It is unlikely that this rather rash action was authorized by Kett or his council of governors, and Sotherton records that the act was carried out by *'a wretched rebell, one Cayme of Bongege although there would have bin given C li (£100) for his life, nothwithstanding hee had the like reward within a month after'*.

That night, as darkness fell, Northampton and his captains made their preparations to defend the city. Great bonfires were built in the market place, where the majority of the army was stationed, and at various guarded points throughout the city. Patrols marched through the darkened streets and strongpoints constructed to deny the rebels entry to the heart of the city. Then, at midnight, alarms rang out as rebels, dodging in and out of the darkened alleys and by-ways, made attacks upon the patrols. Northampton and his deputies were hastily roused from their slumbers and, armed for battle, they sped to the market place from where they despatched additional men to the threatened areas of the city.

Fighting continued throughout the early hours with, according to Neville's account, over 300 people being killed in the confused melees. From the temporary headquarters in the market place it was suggested, by Northampton's friend Lord Sheffield, that they would be best served by constructing ramparts along the eastern edge of the city where the only protection was the easily crossed river. Northampton, convinced by Lord Sheffield's argument, despatched him to carry out the plan with all haste. As the night wore on the fighting subsided and Northampton once more found himself in control of the city.

Lord Sheffield, accompanied by troops and as many labourers as he could muster, made his way through the darkness to the riverside where he supervised the construction of the ramparts. Rebuilding, strengthening and extending the earthworks thrown up by the city authorities they hoped to block the rebels eastern approach to the city. Here, no doubt reassured by the lull in the skirmishing, they set to their task and by eight the next morning the ramparts were almost complete. Sheffield, happy that all was as it should be, retired to the Maids Head tavern where he took breakfast.

As Lord Sheffield emerged, well fed and contented, from the warm interior of the tavern he caught sight of the Herald and a trumpeter riding through Tombland. Upon questioning the Herald, Sheffield discovered that Northampton had received information that four or five hundred rebels were presenting themselves at the Pockthorpe gate and asking to accept the Kings pardon. Happy at the joyful news Sheffield decided to accompany the Herald in person and left his deputies to oversee the final work on the riverside ramparts.

Arriving at the Pockthorpe gate, the most north eastern of the city gates, both Sheffield and the Herald were dismayed to find no sign of any rebels either hostile or repentant. Once esconsed in the corner tower, where they joined Sir John Clere and others, the Herald had his trumpeter sound a call. As the sound echoed through the still morning a horseman approached from the direction of the heath. The Herald summoned the horseman, who turned out to be one John Floateman of Beccles, and informed him that if he and his company would submit themselves to the King's will then they would all be pardoned. At this point Floateman was joined by about twenty others from the rebel camp and, according to Sotherton, that *'hee defyde the Lord Leiuetenant* (Northampton) *and seid he was a Traytour nor wulde of his pardon, nor had deservid pardon, but that they were the Kings true subjects...'*

Whether the 'information' received by Northampton about the rebels wish for pardon was a deliberate diversion or just an unhappy coincidence is unknown but at that moment news reached Lord Sheffield and the Herald that the rebels had crossed the river and were attacking the city from the the area of the 'hospital' in Bishopsgate, or Holmstreet as it was then sometimes known. Sheffield realising that if he did not act quickly he would find the rebels between himself and Northampton's main force in the market place, put spur to his horse and hastened back towards Tombland. When he arrived he discovered that the rebels had penetrated as far as the gates of the Bishops palace, where the church of St Martin at Place now stands and a bare few yards from the Maids Head tavern. And a furious fight was now taking place in the streets to the north and east of the Cathedral.

It appears to have been at this point, on the open ground around St Martins church, that Northampton had positioned his guns before they were to be moved to the new earthworks on the riverbank. However, in the disorganised melee now taking place the guns were as good as useless, and where they could have caused massive slaughter against the advancing rebels they seem to have remained silent.

The battle was going badly for the Royal troops and many of them, more used to open warfare than this oversized street brawl, were retiring towards the market place with the rebels hard upon their heels. Lord Sheffield, hoping to stabilise the defences, gathered a body of the mounted mercenaries, or 'lance knights' as they were known, and led them in a charge along the edge of the Cathedral precincts, past St Martin at Place church, and into Bishopsgate street. The rebels, finding themselves opposed by well trained and vicious cavalry in the tight packed streets, soon began to yield the ground they had taken.

Then at the corner by the hospital Lord Sheffield, still at the head of his troops, floundered with his horse into a ditch. Here, as he tried to disentangle himself from his horse and escape the muddy ditch Sheffield was struck down by one 'Fulke a butcher and carpenter by trade'. Removing his helmet to reveal his identity Sheffield obviously hoped to be taken captive and ransomed by the victorious rebels but Fulke and his comrades, overblown with victory, simply took the opportunity to bludgeon the nobleman to death in the muddy ditch.

With Lord Sheffield now lying dead in the ditch and the blood of their comrades smearing the cobbled street, the heart seems to have gone out of the Royal troops and they began a general withdrawal towards the main market place where Northampton waited with the rest of his troops. The rebels appear to have allowed the retreat to take place virtually unmolested and at about midday the fighting gradually died away. The running battle had lasted several hours and although desperate at times, the casualties appear to have been very light indeed. Sotherton

claims that only forty men died while King Edward's account lists Northampton's
losses as one hundred dead and thirty captured.

As his beaten and demoralised troops began to trail back into the market place
Northampton was left in a very difficult position. His mercenaries seemed to have
little stomach for the street fighting and he had few other troops to send to stem
the rebels advance. If he chose to counter attack, a course of action that would
have been costly in the confined streets, he faced another night of constant
harassment from the rebels already secreted within the walls. No doubt tired by
the night's alarms and disheartened by the death of his friend, Northampton chose
to withdraw.

Northampton, at the head of his tired and defeated troops, withdrew almost
immediately from the city in good order and made for Cambridge. However, news
of the Marquises retreat was met with panic by the loyal citizens of Norwich and
many of them, fearing a general riot by the victorious rebels, chose to flee with the
troops. As Sotherton recounts '*departid divers Cytezins and mens servants ageine to
London ward, and that by certen mens houses of worshippe from which houses every man
made away that they had both plate, mony, and stuffe, and the Cytezins did the like,
some in wells, some in ponds and other secret places..... In which conficte there departid
with them many that had wives and children, some that were with childe, some that were
sicke and deseasid, which were fayne to leave them all, and fled in theyr doublet and
hosen and some in theyr lightest garments beste escape and make haste away...*'

With the retreat of the army of the Marquis of Northampton and the death of
Lord Sheffield, the rebels once more found themselves in control of the city of
Norwich. They had stood up for what they believed was right and defied the
authority of the King's council. They believed that they had shown themselves to
be a force to be reckoned with and could not be simply pushed aside with sweet
words and a show of force. The night after Northamptons retreat the joyful rebels
set fire to some of the houses in Bishopsgate; the gate-house at Bishops bridge; and
the gates at Pockthorpe, Magdalen, St Augustines, Coslaney and Ber street. Along
with these they burnt part of the hospital and in their reverie set fires in many
other places throughout the city as they looted the houses of the rich townspeople.
The rebels, impudent in victory, believed that they could do much as they wished.
However, the wiser heads amongst them must have realised that having sown the
wind they would, in turn, reap the whirlwind.

And now began the Rebellis againe to possess the Cittye and to have Aldermen and Constables att their commandments and in tyme of raine in the night season they incampid in the Cathedral church called Christ's church in Norwich and had the rewle to doe what them listed and kept the gates themselves....

Nicholas Sotherton - The Commoyson in Norfolk

The night of the rebels re-entry into Norwich was not a peaceful one for its inhabitants. Many of the more prosperous residents, or those with a reason to fear the rebel recapture of the city, had fled towards London and Cambridge with the army of Northampton. For those that remained within the city walls many of their worst fears were to become a reality within a very short space of time.

The disorganised rabble of rebels poured into the now defenceless city and began to rampage through the near deserted streets in search of mischief and mayhem. Fires had been set at several of the city gates and parts of Holmfirth street (Bishopsgate) and the hospital were also in flames. No one within the city walls seems to have been safe from the vengeance of the rebels' and looting of shops and warehouses was commonplace. Sotherton recounts that the rebels *'entrid every man's howse and spoylid all they could come by in so much that, thowgh the most parte of the best of the Cyttie were departid as is aforesayde, yeat the servants of the seid Cytezins to save ye rest of theyr Master's goods devisid to bake bred and to rost, bake pasties and give it unto them to save the rest....'*

Augustine Steward, the Mayors deputy, had remained in the city after the departure of Northampton and his army and, although he had been acting on the orders of the Mayor whom Kett still had control of, he appears to have been singled out for the attention of the rebels. Firstly a company of rebels came battering upon his gates searching for Northampton and his officers who had lodged there the previous night. Finding that their quarry had fled and having ransacked the house Steward was obliged to give them all the money he had in his purse to convince them to leave his house. This first company had barely departed when they were followed by a second group who, less keen on finding prisoners and more keen on looting, broke open Stewards shop and began to carry out the stock of cloth that was stored there. Upon being harangued by one of their own company, a servant of Mr Smith of Huntingfields named Doo, that they *'should all bee hangid'* for their crimes the rebels then returned the stolen goods but not before they had forced Steward to *'cutt both shirt cloaths and doublet cloths of fustian and given them to save ye rest'*.

Steward's troubles were not over for as soon as this second company had departed, no doubt happy with their 'bargains', a third company of rebels appeared at his shop. Intent on doing mischief this third group were only appeased when the resourceful Doo once again stepped into the breach. Explaining that the shop had already been ransacked and stripped of its goods he convinced them, with the aid of three or four others, to move on and leave Steward in peace.

Steward's troubles were echoed all through the city streets and as darkness fell and the fires brought under control the citizens of Norwich cowered behind their barred and bolted doors as the rebels rampaged through the streets. Eventually the situation seems to have been brought under control by the rebel 'governors' and, once more in control, they set to organising themselves. Watches were stationed on the city gates and patrols sent through the streets to keep order while many of the rebels, trying to avoid the uncomfortable heavy dews that they had suffered while camping on the heath, took to camping out in the nave of the Cathedral.

For Robert Kett and the other leaders of the rebellion the period after the recapture of Norwich must have been a difficult and trying time. Their followers, full of the invincible confidence that comes with victory, must have been difficult to control and no doubt committed many crimes that their leaders would have perceived as folly. However, Kett and the governors were only able to remain as leaders of the rebellion if they had the support of their followers. Becoming unpopular with the mass of the rebels would lead to their immediate overthrow and replacement by those more amenable to the rebels wishes. On the other hand they also had to show themselves to be powerful and decisive or they would leave themselves open to charges of collaboration with the authorities, and of general weakness. Kett found himself walking a tightrope with the rebels on one side and the best interests of the rebellion on the other.

Kett also had other very pressing matters on his mind at that moment. Having defeated the Marquis of Northampton and sent his Royal forces hotfooting it back to Cambridge he now faced a very grave situation. The government in London could not allow such actions to go unpunished and Kett realised that it was only a matter of time before a new and more powerful army was sent against him. If he succeeded in defeating another Royal force then a third would be sent. The government could not be seen to be beaten by these East Anglian rebels and would do anything within their power to put an end to the rebellion; at whatever cost.

At this point in the rebellion Kett had only two routes open to him that could lead to a favourable outcome for the rebels. Firstly he could gather his forces camped around Norwich and march on London. Hopefully gathering support from the other rebel camps dotted throughout East Anglia en route he could advance upon the capital and plead his case for reform from a position of strength outside the walls of London itself. With the rest of the country in ferment it would be unlikely that a large enough force to stop him could be gathered at short notice. With extra support from the camps at Bury St Edmunds and Melton he could probably muster a force at least twice the size of the largest government army available.

Ketts second course of action was much simpler. By remaining where they were the rebels held one of England's major cities, and much of the countryside around it, in their grasp. By expanding their uprising outwards from this central point they could extend their control to cover all of Norfolk and probably most of East Anglia as well. Risings were already taking place in much of the region and by simply co-ordinating what was already happening and expanding to cover the areas still controlled by the local authorities, Kett hoped to be able to cause a popular rising throughout the eastern region. If such a rising took place the government would see it as the general will of the people rather than a limited rebellion and have to come to terms or suffer the consequences.

For Kett the first option, a general march on London, was by far the least attractive of the two ideas. It contained so many variables, relying as it did on the general will of the people, that it would be difficult and highly dangerous to carry out. The rebels, all fired with enthusiasm after recapturing Norwich, would undoubtedly follow him at first but, with harvest time fast approaching and the memory of previous year's empty bellies, it was all too likely that their numbers would diminish as the year progressed and they marched further and further away from their own homes. With the French and Scots ready to invade, a general march on London could easily be seen as a treasonous act against the monarch; a monarch they had all sworn that they were loyal to. No, for Kett and his governors a march on London was not a real option; far better to remain where he was and spread his message throughout the rest of the eastern counties. Let the government come to him.

Kett's main objective after the defeat of Northampton was to secure the other major towns in Norfolk that still held out against the rebels. With this in mind, on the 5th of August, Robert Kett and his fellow govenors drew up a commission to send troops against Great Yarmouth. At this time Yarmouth was the second largest town in the county and a prosperous seaport that was home to a nationally important fishing fleet. The town had already seen off one contingent of rebels who had crossed the border from Suffolk and with stout and maintained walls of over a mile in length the task of taking the town could not be lightly undertaken. However, as Kett's commission makes clear, the rebels believed that the arrival of an armed body of men claiming to act in the interests of the monarchy would be enough to secure them entry to the town.

> *Be it known to all men, that we Robert Kett and Thomas Aldrich, commissioners of the King's Camp at Mousehold, have appointed out of our camp aforesaid, one hundred men to return from us to Yarmouth, for the maintenance of the King's town there against our enemies. Also we do certify you, that we, for the more sufficient and necessary victualling of our said one hundred men, do appoint Richard Smith, Thomas Clarke and John Rotherham, and also to take up horses for the further aiding of our said men. Dated at the King's Great Camp at Mousehold the 5th day of August in the third year of the reign of our sovereign Lord King Edward the Sixth.*

That same day, the 5th of August, the hundred men under the nominal command of one Nicholas Byron set out from the heath towards Great Yarmouth. However Kett's early hopes of the town opening its gates before them and joining with the rebels were sadly mistaken. The town councillors, perhaps strengthened by the thought of Vice Admiral Wodehouse patrolling the sea to their rearward, denied the rebels entry and sent them packing back towards their 'great camp' on Mousehold. This rejection, although a blow to the rebels hopes of a peaceful expansion of the uprising, simply strengthened their resolve.

Nearly a fortnight after their first attempt upon Yarmouth, on August 17th, a second attempt was made to secure the town for the rebels. A large force of rebels had been detached from the main body of the army and been sent towards the coast. Their first target was the smaller fishing port of Lowestoft which they took without trouble. Here they acquired cannons, probably by unmounting them from small ships in the harbour, which they took with them in their attempt on the defences of Yarmouth. On the 17th the rebels opened fire on several of the towns stout gate-houses but, due to the ferocity of the town's own cannon fire, they were forced to withdraw.

While the rebels regrouped and licked their wounds before commencing another attack the townsfolk are said to have devised a plan to outwit the rebels. Between the rebel positions and the town walls stood a great stack of hay that had been harvested and now stood drying in the sun. Upon the rebels advance the townsfolk set fire to the hay which, being fanned by a northerly wind, blew thick smoke into the faces of the advancing soldiers. Under cover of this early 'smokescreen' the town's soldiers advanced in a surprise attack upon the rebel lines and, catching the rebels off guard, managed to capture thirty of their soldiers and six guns. These they took with them as they beat a hasty retreat back behind the defensive walls of the town.

The rebels, angered at the loss of the guns they had only just captured from Lowestoft and embarrassed by the ease with which they had been duped, seem to have abandoned all attempts at capturing the town. Instead, no doubt galled by the townspeople's actions, the rebels set about causing the town as much damage as they could. Firstly the rebels set fire to much of the building material, designed for use in the new harbour, that had been left unprotected outside the town walls. Not content with this act of wanton destruction they then attacked the town's south gate where they proceeded to cause as much damage as possible. This action was brought to a halt only when the rebels were driven back by the well directed fire of the town's artillery. Now thwarted on all fronts the rebels lost heart and marched away to rejoin the main rebel force at Norwich. Yarmouth, still safe behind its defences, was left in peace for the remainder of the rebellion.

The failure of the rebels to capture Great Yarmouth and their subsequent failure to spread the rebellion beyond the immediate area of Norwich and the other camps was a serious blow to Kett's hopes. His plans relied upon being able to take the relatively small scale uprising and turn it into a nationwide movement. If he failed in this then the whole rebellion, and in particular its leaders, would be doomed. In London, events were moving on apace; a new army was being gathered and Robert Kett was running out of time.

The events now taking place in London, under the direction of Protector Somerset and the council, were almost as frantic as the events taking place in East Anglia. The council had met to discuss the situation in Norfolk on the 3rd of August; only two days after Northampton's ignominious retreat towards Cambridge and two days before the rebels first attempt on Yarmouth. They were being kept informed of events at a local level by many of the town councillors of the region who still remained loyal to the Crown and had, in fact, received petitions from Yarmouth after the rebels first attempt on the town. For once understanding the urgency of the situation, and realising that they had to act quickly before Kett managed to spread the rebellion, the council drew up plans to despatch a second, much larger, army to the region.

This new army consisted of a hard core of professional soldiers paid for by the Crown and, according to the Royal accounts, numbering 7500 men of whom 1500 were cavalry. They were drawn from many sources and the bulk of the cavalry was again made up of foreign mercenaries. This central division was to be supplemented by soldiers drawn from the loyal areas of East Anglia and was to join with the remnants of Northampton's forces at Cambridge. The army in total probably consisted of between 10,000 and 14,000 men and was placed, by the 15th of August, under the sole command of the Earl of Warwick.

Warwick, a veteran campaigner, was probably one of the most able soldiers in England at the time and was, later that year, to overthrow Somerset as leader of the council. At the time of his appointment as commander of the East Anglian army Warwick was marching north with a detachment of soldiers to keep a check on the many small uprisings that were occurring throughout the country. His main concern after his appointment appears to have been the gathering of sufficient numbers of troops to quell the rebellion and on August the 15th a proclamation was issued.

> 'The Kings Majesty, by the advice of his most entirely beloved uncle the Lord Protector, and the rest of his highness' council, straightly chargeth and commandeth all gentlemen, of what estate, degree, or condition soever they be, who hath their habitation and dwelling in Essex, to depart from the court and the City of London and other places near unto them into their several habitations in the said county of Essex with all convenient speed, there to remain till they shall know further of the King's majesties pleasure; likewise all such gentlemen as hath their habitations and dwellings in Suffolk, to depart unto their said habitations in Suffolk and there to remain until such time as they shall have commandment from the Kings majesty or from the Earl of Warwick; and further that all gentlemen inhabitants of Norfolk do repair to the said Earl of Warwick so that they be with the said Earl to attend upon him in the King's majesty's army in his conduct and leading, for his highness' better service, upon Saturday next following, or Sunday at the furthest.'

Warwick, with his army now swollen by the local gentry and their armed retainers, was in Cambridge by the 20th of August where he was joined by

Northampton and his troops. From here the army marched into Norfolk reaching Wymondham, the birthplace of the rebellion, on the 22nd. Here the army received more support in the shape of Lord Willoughby of Parham and several other members of the East Anglian gentry and their followers. The following day, the 23rd, Warwick and the army continued their march towards Norwich eventually halting at Intwood Hall, home of Sir Thomas Gresham and three miles from the city walls. Some of the army units seem to have advanced still further and by the evening of the 23rd the rebels in Norwich, by climbing the many church towers and steeples, could plainly make out the Royal army in the distance.

That evening, as the Royal army camped within sight of the rebels, Sotherton claims that Robert Kett himself took the opportunity to climb one of the steeples in the city to view the advancing menace. It is likely that Kett already knew the strength of Warwicks army and no doubt realised that this was by no means going to be as simple as it had been upon Northampton's approach to the city those few short weeks before. Warwick had an army of almost equal strength to Ketts. His troops were, in the main, professional soldiers and his orders were, no doubt, specific. One way or another the rebellion must end.

*Whylst theis things were a doeing and that the King was advertisid of theyr
doeings that by noe meanis they would avert from theyer rebellion, and that
noe pardon would bee receidid, the King sent into Lincolnshire and other
placis of the Realme and mustridd and toke up a greate numbre of souldiours
and allsoe sent for divers Launce Knights and other strangers to make a
power to suppres the seide rebells....*
Nicholas Sotherton - The Commoyson in Norfolk

On the morning of the 24th of August 1549 over 24,000 armed men were
camped in and around the ancient walled city of Norwich. These two great
armies, both swearing allegiance to the same young boy who was their King, were
both preparing for a meeting that would decide, one way or another, the final
outcome of Kett's rebellion.

That morning, after passing the night at Intwood House, Warwick and his fellow
officers proceeded to Norwich where they drew up their forces within a mile of the
walls facing St Stephens gate. According to Sotherton Warwick *'of his clemencie
and for avoiding of bloudshed and saving the gentlemen in captivity'* sent forward his
Herald, Gilbert Dethick, to summon the city to open its gates and allow him entry.
The Herald's message reached the ears of Robert Kett, who appears to have left
Mount Surrey and entered the city. Upon his orders Augustine Steward and
Robert Rugge, another former Mayor of Norwich, went out to meet the Herald.

The meeting with the Herald appears to have been one of political manoeuvring
and it does shed some light upon the thoughts that must have been going through
the rebel's minds at the time. Steward and Rugge asked the Herald to state his
business and the Herald, in turn, asked them for permission for his master, the
Earl of Warwick, to enter the city. Steward and Rugge then said that they would
rather let Warwick enter the city gates than receive a *'greate summe of mony'* but that
it was beyond their power. Rather they thought the Herald had come once more
to offer pardon to those rebels that would receive it. This was obviously not within
the Herald's remit but, upon the suggestion, he returned to Warwick to put the idea
to him. Warwick, seeing the golden opportunity of a bloodless end to the rebellion
thrust into his hands, agreed to the suggestion and the Herald once more returned
to the gates.

The very fact that both Steward and Rugge made the suggestion of offering the rebels pardon indicates that the idea of a surrender on good terms had, in fact, come from Kett and was high on his personal agenda. He realised that the armies were well matched (in numbers if not experience) and that open hostility would end in much bloodshed. So, he was giving Warwick the opportunity to end it quickly and honourably with no loss of life on either side. It is most unlikely that either Steward or Rugge would have acted upon their own authority. The very fact that it was these two, both respected members of the lawful city authorities, that were sent to negotiate indicates that Kett wished to show Warwick that he was in earnest.

Gilbert Dethick the Herald and a trumpeter returned to St Stephens gate where they were met by Steward and Rugge. Escorted by thirty or forty rebel horsemen, riding before them two by two, the Herald was led through the streets of Norwich, past the stark remains of the burnt buildings in Holmstreet and out the eastern side of the city at Bishops bridge. Here the trumpeter sounded several blasts upon his horn to summon the rebels. In a very short space of time the hillside before them became a seething mass of people as the rebels came down from their camp on the heath to hear the Herald's proclamation. With the rebels now assembled and great shouts of 'God save King Edward' rising from the ranks, the Herald and his trumpeter, accompanied by Steward and Rugge made their way *through ye ranks quietly the space of a quarter of a myle*. Here, upon a small hill amid the rebel ranks, the Herald read his offer of pardon to the crowd.

The Herald's message, however, was not to the liking of the rebels gathered before him. It started sweetly enough by stating that the King had sent forth the Earl of Warwick to offer pardon to *'his naturall subjects'* and if they would humbly submit themselves to the King's mercy then both their life and goods would be spared. However, the message continued that if they refused, then the Earl of Warwick would never *'depart out of the place till without pitty and mercy hee had vanquished them with the sword'*. It was also pointed out that the pardon applied only to the general mass of the rebels and that Robert Kett was to be exempted.

Although some of the rebels found the offer of a general pardon acceptable the vast majority seem to have been angered by the Herald's harsh tones and many, perhaps rightly, suspected that the kind words of the moment would not match the harsh reactions of the county's gentry after the mob had dispersed. Things were rapidly getting out of hand on the hillside. Shouts went up that the Herald was a traitor; that he was not a genuine Herald at all but rather *'made by the Gentlemen putting on him a piece of an old cope* (church vestment) *for his cote armour'*. Threats rang through the crowd and the Herald and trumpeter began to fear for their own safety. It was at this point, just as the Herald began to understand the true power of this group of disgruntled individuals, the Robert Kett made his appearance.

Until then it seems that Kett had stayed away from the meeting but now, when his arrival and subsequent subduing of the crowd could do most to impress the Herald with his power, he put in his appearance. With Kett acting as escort the Herald was taken to another section of the hillside where he could repeat his offer. Now, although probably ordered by Warwick to show Kett no signs of any special recognition of his position, the Herald was forced to seek the protection of Kett and his authority.

During this second reading of Warwick's offer of pardon an event took place that, as far as the vast majority of the rebels were concerned, dispelled any scant chances of a peaceful end to the uprising. As the Herald shouted forth his proclamation he was heckled by a young lad in the crowd who made insulting gestures and, it is said, bared his buttocks at the King's representative. This foolish horseplay soon got out of hand as recounted by Sotherton. *'Before the end thereof* (the Heralds message) *for that an ungracious ladd on the other syde had turnid his tayle to them above that one with a corrier shot att him and slew him wherewith came riding through the wood a xii or more horsemen exclaiming that the Harrold cam not but for a traine to have them all destroyid....'*

The shooting of the boy with the 'corrier', a type of handgun, is traditionally meant to have been committed by one of Warwick's troops but, as Warwick was encamped on the other side of the city (with the river between the two sides) and the fact that it is stated several times that the Herald and trumpeter came alone, we must assume that the foul deed was committed by a rebel sympathetic to the slight done to the Herald's dignity. Whatever the truth of the matter, the incident put an end to all possibilities of a general pardon being accepted by the mass of the rebels. However, Kett may have had very different ideas indeed.

Now, as the rebel army upon the hillside yelled forth their fury at the slaying of the young lad, the Herald attempted to withdraw back into the relative safety of the city. In this move he was accompanied by Robert Kett who was, according to Sotherton, *'willing to have gone with the Herald to the Lord Leiuetenant'*. It appears that Kett, even after the scene on the hillside, was still willing to try and negotiate a peaceful end to the uprising. Kett's plan to accompany the Herald soon came to nothing as, down from the heath, came a body of horsemen. These men hastened after Kett and the Herald and, halting them, demanded *'Whither away? Whither away, Mr Kett? If you goe, wee will goe with you, and with you will live and dye'*. These fine words can be seen as a statement of the rebels loyalty to Kett but, just as easily and perhaps more in keeping with the context of events, they can also be read as the rebels being unwilling to let Kett depart alone to negotiate on their behalf.

At this point the Herald, seeing that a large number of the disgruntled rebels were now advancing to join the debate, urged Kett to return to the hillside and pacify the rebels gathered there. Kett really had very little choice in the matter and, as the Herald rode back to Warwick through the streets of Norwich, Kett was escorted by his 'loyal' horsemen back to the hillside. With the departure of the Herald went the last chance that Kett had of negotiating a surrender.

Although at this point in the uprising Robert Kett appears to have been in favour of a negotiated settlement his sentiments were not shared by the vast majority of the rebel army. The defeat of Northampton's army had obviously filled them with confidence and their subsequent treatment by Warwick's Herald had put them in a belligerent mood. Feeling that they were more than a match for the advancing Royal army, many of the rebels, probably acting on their own initiative, re-entered the city of Norwich and prepared to defend it against the Earl of Warwick.

Upon the Herald's return to his position the Earl of Warwick, realising that the negotiations would go no further, decided to act quickly and, with luck, decisively. Bringing his artillery forward he established his guns somewhere in the region of the leper house on the London road and opened fire upon St Stephens gates. In a matter of minutes the portcullis of the gate-house had been battered down and a strong force, led by Northampton and Captain Thomas Drury, had entered the city and engaged the rebels in the area of Needham street (todays St Stephens street). The fighting was hard and, for a while, it seemed that the rebels may have been able to expel the soldiers from the city. Then, as Warwick, feared an early reverse, news reached him from Augustine Steward.

Within the city, things were in confusion. The rebels were busy defending he area around St Stephens gate and seem to have paid little attention to the rest of the loyal inhabitants of Norwich. Steward, acting with his accustomed resolve, passed word to Warwick that the Brazen gate, the gate directly to the south of St Stephens, was in poor repair and could easily be broken down. At one and the same time Steward informed the Earl that he had managed to secure and open the Westwick, or St Benedicts, gate. Warwick seized the opportunity.

Leaving his guns to support Northampton's attack he sent his pioneers, supported no doubt with extra troops, to try their luck in opening the Brazen gates while he, with the bulk of his force hastened to the north and the open Westwick gate. The pioneers were quickly successful and forced open the gates allowing more troops into the city. With Warwick now advancing along St Benedicts Street and Pottergate, Northampton and Drury in Needham Street (St Stephens) and a third force advancing in the region of St Wynwaloys Street (All Saint's Green), the rebels had no option other than retreat.

In a matter of minutes all resistance to Warwicks forces in the western half of the city had ceased and the rebels were in headlong flight back towards the river. Some rebels, however, were not quick enough to retire and when Warwick, marching from the north, arrived in the main market place he managed to capture a group of forty nine rebel soldiers who were, no doubt, retreating from the attacks from the south. In an act of calculated brutality Warwick immediately had all forty nine of his prisoners strung up in the market place. This act seems to have had the desired effect and soon hundreds of the citizens of Norwich emerged from their houses to shout forth their loyalty to the Crown and seek the Earl's pardon. '*To whome*', according to Sotherton, '*the Lord Leiutenant answrid they should have pardon and commandid every man home to his howse and keepe the same that noe Rebel were therein sustained which made a greate nombre of glad hartis..*'

Now that Warwick had made an inroad upon the city and captured most of the area to the south of the Wensum, he was faced with the same dilemma that had faced both Northampton and the rebels before him. How best to hold on to the territory without suffering massive casualties. However, before Warwick could put any plans into effect he suffered a reverse in his fortunes that once more gave heart to the rebel cause.

At about three o'clock that same afternoon, the 24th of August, the last remnants of Warwick's army were entering the city via the Westwick Gate. This last convoy, consisting mainly of the artillery train and its associated supply wagons, was in the charge of a group of Welsh wagon masters. These men, not knowing the city and possibly misunderstanding their orders, proceeded along St Benedicts Street and, instead of turning right to take them to the market square and the safety of the rest of the assembled army, continued east towards Tombland. Now, with the guns in an area of the city only nominally controlled by the Earl, the rebels saw their chance and seized upon it.

The rebels now assembled 'a grete company' in the area of Tombland and the Cathedral. From here they split into three units which, advancing up St Michaels

Street, Middle Wymer Street and St Peter Hungate Street (Elm Hill, Princes Street and Queen Street) hoped to cut off the artillery convoy. Upon gathering in the area of St Andrews Hall the rebels fell upon a band of Warwicks soldiers and killed three or four '*Gentyllmen*'. Warwick, hearing the uproar taking place a few streets away, sent troops to investigate and a brisk fight started around St Andrews with volleys of arrows being exchanged at very short range. This small battle was finally concluded when Captain Drury, leading a body of handgunners, appeared upon the scene and '*dischargid on such a sudden that the seid Rebellis recoylid whereat they were soe hastily pursuid that many of them were feine to take churchyards and hyd under the wallis and fell flat in the allies*'.

For Drury and his men fighting in the confined alleys around Elm Hill must have been a nightmare of confusion. However, the superior firepower and discipline of the Royal troops soon began to take their toll and the rebels were forced back towards Bishopsgate Street. The fight lasted no more than half an hour and Sotherton claims that over a hundred died in the firefight with Neville giving the number at three times as many. Whatever the true figure the rebels were now fleeing the city with Drury and his men hot on their heels.

While this fight was taking place the train of artillery, seemingly oblivious to the commotion behind it, had entered Bishopsgate Street. With few guards it stood little chance when, down from the heath, a large group of rebels, led by Miles the rebel master gunner, crossed Bishops Bridge and captured it. The Welshmen, heavily outnumbered, quickly retired and during the fight the King's master gunner was slain. The fight put up by the Welshmen was, according to Nevilles account, '*cowardly*' and his description of the Welsh acting '*like Sheep*' was so offensive that it was cut out of all but the earliest editions of his work. With the guns and powder now in the rebel's hands they attempted to transport it back over the bridge and up to the safety of the heath. However, before they were entirely clear of the city they were intercepted by the soldiers under the command of Captain Drury who, having chased the first attackers away, now set to regaining the guns.

Drury's brave action managed to salvage at least some of the wagons although, according to Sotherton's account, only at the expense of a '*grett losse of men*'. The rest; the guns, shot, powder and general supplies were carried off to the camp on the heath; there to be put to good use against their original owners.

That evening, as the sun set on the newly captured city, the Earl and his officers retired to the relative comfort of Augustine Steward's house and there laid their plans. The watch was set about the city and Lord Willoughby was commanded to guard the Bishopsgate gate-house and bridge which, from experience, the Earl recognised as the city's weakest point. Once the watch was set, his men accommodated in the houses of the citizens and all relatively quite within the city, Warwick retired for the night.

Then, at about ten in the evening, the streets came alive once more with the shouts of 'fire'. The rebels had again managed to enter the city, this time through the Conisford or South Gates, and had there set several houses on fire along what is now King Street. The fire soon spread amid the grain stores and warehouses that made up many of the buildings in that part of the city until there was burnt, according to Sotherton, '*a whole parish or two on both sides the way*'. Warwick, hastily summing up the situation, immediately despatched troops to eject the rebels which they achieved with little difficulty. However, wary of the cunning of the rebel leaders, Warwick was loath to send additional troops to help extinguish the fires now raging in that area of the city as he feared that the whole venture was simply a rebel scheme to divert troops away from the north of the city which would then be vulnerable to another assault.

As night descended on the city Warwick once more returned to the house of Augustine Steward, where the Earl's banner of the bear and ragged staff now hung limply above the doorway, to pass what few hours of darkness remained in a fitful slumber. He was now the sole commander of a besieged city. A city that had suffered at the hands of both sides and, most likely, would suffer further torments the following day. Outside, in the city streets, the night sky was lit with the flames from the fires that still raged in the area of the Conisford gate while, on the dark mound that was the heath, the rebels rested and awaited the coming of the dawn.

The next daye Sundaye in ye morning went every one to armour, when though for the largenes of the Citty and difficilitie thereof the Lord Leiuetenant was by ye best advisid to depart til furder puissance, yeat valiantly answerid by God's grace not to depart the Cittye but would deliver it or leave his life...'

Nicholas Sotherton - The Commoyson in Norfolk

As the sun rose the next morning, the 25th of August, the bells of the dozens of Norwich churches rang out to welcome in the Sabbath. However, with the smoke from burning houses still hanging in the cool morning air, this Sunday was unlikely to prove a peaceful day of rest for any who now awoke within the battered city walls.

At first light the Royal soldiers were armed and abroad in the city streets preparing for whatever the day might bring. The citizens of Norwich, however, were somewhat less keen on the way in which things appeared to be turning out. As far as they were concerned the Earl of Warwick was now in much the same position as Northampton had been in at the end of the previous month. They could foresee another series of rebel assaults on the city, and the consequential damage to their homes and property, and would rather be left in the hands of the rebels than become a battleground to be fought over once again.

These sentiments were transmitted to the Earl early that Sunday morning and the leading citizens of Norwich made it plain to Warwick that they would rather see him withdraw now, before more damage was caused, than be driven out by the rebels. The Earl, confident in his soldiers ability and his own skills as a general, would have none of it and, in a speech before the City's representatives, plainly stated that he would not desert them and would, if occasion necessitated, lay down his own life rather than withdraw. In addition the Earl, now fired by his own rhetoric, convinced the citizens to swear upon their own swords and upon the cross that they too would lay down their lives rather than see the rebels retake the city.

With these fiery words and bold sentiments still ringing loudly in the ears of citizens and soldiers alike, news arrived that the rebels had once more begun an assault upon the city. This attack was unlike those that had gone before it and marked a dramatic change in the tactics adopted by the rebels. Seeing that the Bishopsgate was now heavily defended and that the attack on the southern Conisford gate had not drawn Warwick forth, the rebels made a concerted attack upon the northern edge of the city. Bringing up several of their, by now numerous, cannon the rebel gunners bombarded an area of wall located somewhere between the Magdalen gate and the Pockthorpe gate and in a short space of time had created a breach large enough to enter the city. The rebel troops hurriedly advanced through the ruined wall and, meeting with little resistance, soon occupied most of the area known as 'Norwich over the water'.

This area of the city, located to the north of the Wensum, was connected to the main city centre by four bridges. Unwilling, or unable, to withdraw troops from the Bishopsgate area to clear the area of 'Norwich over' that the rebels now occupied, Warwick decided his best course of action probably lay in confining the rebel incursion and stopping them moving further south. With this in mind Warwick ordered the destruction of the four bridges across the Wensum which, if it had been carried out, would have split the city into a rebel sector and a Royal sector. Although this plan seems to have been put into action and at least one of the bridges, Whitefriars, completely destroyed the job was never completed. At the insistent requests of the leading citizens of Norwich, probably seeing further rebuilding expenses, Warwick was convinced to leave the other three bridges intact.

Now, with 'Norwich over' still largely in rebel hands, Warwick had little choice but to send in his reserve troops, until then stationed in the market place, and clear the rebels out of the city street by street. Among these was, once again, Captain Drury and his unit of handgunners who, no doubt, were considered more suitable for this type of street clearing operation after their previous success. The fighting was difficult and costly to both sides but eventually the rebels were forced back and, according to Sotherton, *'in there repuls was many slaine'*. The casualties, however, were not confined simply to the ranks of the rebels. In the churchyard of St Martin at Place were buried one George Hastings along with three of Captain Drury's handgunners and another un-named gentlemen; all casualties of Warwicks counter attack across the bridges.

With 'Norwich over' now back under his control Warwick was again faced with the task of defending an extended perimeter. A perimeter that, in many areas, now resembled more of a builders yard than a defensive line. The breach in the wall, through which the rebels had entered the city, was only one part of the problem. Previous attacks made by the rebels, including those that had driven Northampton from the city, had left most of the north and east facing gate-houses in a very poor state of repair. Many of the gates were either badly damaged or weakened by fire and Warwicks only answer was to amass large bodies of soldiers at each threatened spot in the defences and deter the rebels from attacking by sheer force of numbers.

Although this tactic seems to have worked it must have been a severe strain upon the Earl's limited resources. He could hardly withdraw men from the riverside by Bishopsgate without leaving the area once more open to attack and even with the help of the, by now, armed citizens, Warwick's reserves must have been all but depleted. With Bishopsbridge and its gate-house under constant artillery bombardment from the captured guns on the heath, Warwick must have desperately felt the need of reinforcements.

The bombardment of Bishopsgate was becoming a very serious threat to the city. The captured Royal guns and ammunition had been put to good use and, under the experienced eye of Miles the rebel master gunner, the damage being caused by the accurate shooting was beginning to mount. Finally, after many hours of constant battering, one of the towers of the gate-house at Bishops bridge succumbed to the rebel shots and collapsed. Although not clearing the way for an assault this small victory must have lifted the hearts of many of the watching rebels and, according to Sotherton, *'slew many men that there gardid'*. Now, with Warwick's troops spread too thinly throughout the city and the continued bombardment of Bishopsbridge, the recapture of the city by the rebels appeared to be only a matter of time.

The rest of that long Sunday afternoon the rebel bombardment of the city continued without any sign of it diminishing. The Royal troops around Bishopsbridge had no choice but to sit behind their newly constructed ramparts and take the battering that the rebels handed out to them. With the bombarding guns high on the heath Warwick's troops were in no position to be able to return their fire and with so many troops now tied up defending the breached walls and gates to the north of the Wensum, Warwick did not have the reserves to sally out from the city and clear the gun positions. As the powder smoke rolled lazily down the hill from the heath and the long afternoon gradually faded into the late summer evening it appeared that, saving further developments, the scene was set for a long drawn out stalemate.

For once, the night that settled gently over the battered city passed peacefully enough. The rebels, unable to target their guns to any great effect in the darkness, reduced their bombardment to no more than a desultory and sporadic firing that kept the defenders awake and alert. Throughout the city watchfires burnt and patrols marched quietly through the streets preparing for renewed rebel attacks. At the northern gate-houses and the breached walls groups of soldiers gathered together around the great fires for both warmth and comfort and passed the night as best they could. But, as dawn crept stealthily through the streets, like a thief returning to his hideout before daybreak, no attack was forthcoming and the defenders let forth small sighs of relief before recalling their situation and preparing themselves for another days bombardment.

That morning, Monday the 26th of August, passed in much the same manner as the previous afternoon. Officers of the watch made their rounds, relieved guards of their duties and offered words of encouragement to their men while, high on the heath, the rebels once more began their bombardment of the city. In short it became an armed standoff or stalemate with both sides strong enough to hold their relative positions but neither side having the troops to break through the others defences. Then, in the early afternoon as Warwick sat down to a hastily prepared dinner in Augustine Steward's house, the balance of power shifted.

As the Earl sat dining with his officers, accompanied by the sharp crump of the rebel guns, a new sound, the sound of sharp musketry fire, was heard in the distance. Hastily leaving their unfinished meal, and no doubt fearing another rebel assault, the officers quickly departed to learn the source of this new disturbance. However, the Earl's fears of attack were soon proved to be without foundation as the firing came not from the east but from the west. At last, after days of waiting, the Royal reinforcements had arrived within sight of the city walls and, to announce their arrival, were discharging their handguns into the air.

These reinforcements, so badly needed by the Earl, consisted of between a thousand and fifteen hundred foreign 'lance knights', or Landsknechts, who were employed by the government as mercenaries. Accompanied by their families, the approach of the new force from the west must have appeared, at least to those watchers on the heath, to be much greater in number than it actually was. Now, as the gates were flung open in welcome and the mercenaries entered the city, the rebels must have feared that the tide had finally turned against them.

For Warwick the arrival of his reinforcements must have come as a blessed relief. Finally he had the troops not just to secure the city but also to be able to venture forth from the defences in enough strength to either disperse the rebels from their camp or, at the very least, hary their supply lines and cut them off from any further support from the surrounding countryside. With over a thousand additional fully trained and experienced troops the Earl could hold the city indefinitely, cutting off the rebel's access to its supplies and markets, and, by sending out large armed patrols, confine them to their camp.

Kett and the other rebel leaders must have understood just as well as the Earl of Warwick the true significance of the arrival of the 'lance knights'. With over a thousand extra troops behind the defences they now had virtually no chance of retaking the city and were therefore denied access to its supplies. Without these the rebels would have to rely on the surrounding countryside for its day to day needs and, although difficult, living off the land was a possibility. However, this relied on Kett being able to keep the Royal troops stuck behind their barricades. Any advance into the countryside by the Earl's forces would disrupt the rebels remaining supply lines and starvation and defeat would become only a matter of time. Also harvest time was fast approaching and although this would mean better pickings for the rebels the majority of them no doubt had their own harvests to think of. They would be very reluctant to sit outside a besieged city while their own harvests lay wasting in the fields.

Kett now had few choices. He could either continue his siege of the city, thereby risking the gradual decline in the number of his own forces and the very real portability of further Royal reinforcements, or finally draw the situation to a conclusion. A negotiated peace was still a very real possibility but with the belligerent mood of the rebels it was unlikely to be easily achieved. Kett's only other real option lay in attempting to draw out Warwick's forces from the city defences and either defeating them in open battle or, by impressing both his own side and the Earl's with the strength of the opposition, forcing them to negotiate.

At some point on the afternoon of the 26th of August, after the arrival of Warwick's reinforcements, it is supposed that Robert Kett sat down to discuss the military situation with his fellow leaders of the rebellion. The decision reached by the rebel govenors, though far reaching in its consequences, was simple. That night, under cover of the few hours of darkness, the rebels would abandon their camp on the heath, withdraw from Norwich onto the flat plain to the east and, the following day, offer battle to the Earl of Warwick.

Whylst theis things were a doeing was devising in the Rebellis Campe what were best to do for victory, and as they had oft giving themselvis from good admonicion to theyr own wills, soe now, neere unto such tyme as theyr destruction was present, had God suffrid them to bee deludid for now instead of putting theyr trust in God they trustid uppon faynid prophecies....
Nicholas Sotherton - The Commoyson in Norfolk

As the sun went down on the evening of Monday the 25th of August the rebel camp on the heath above Norwich became the scene of determined activity. Robert Kett, supposed leader of the rebel forces, had decided that they should face the army of the Earl of Warwick in one final battle. For the rebels this was the final act of the long drama they had all played their part in. They were going to stand, shoulder to shoulder, against the massed forces of the Crown and, one way or another, the dispute would be settled. Either, faced with the rebels massed ranks, Warwick would re-open negotiations or a battle would be fought in which the winner would stand with right on their side. One way or another the rebellion would end.

That night the rebels abandoned their camp on Mousehold heath. Setting fire to the temporary dwellings they had erected upon the heath's summit, the rebels carried off all their goods, arms and ammunition to the site chosen for their confrontation. With them went the prisoners, until that time held secured in Mount Surrey, and the artillery that they had captured. All, under cover of darkness were transported to their new site; the plain at Dussindale.

The choice of the site by the rebels on which they would confront Warwick's army has always appeared as a bit of a mystery to historians. Today it is generally accepted as being a site about two miles east of the city centre in an area now occupied by a housing estate and St Andrew's hospital. At the time the land surrounding Dussindale would be relatively flat and generally open with few enclosure hedges or fences. This fact makes the site obviously advantageous to the large amounts of cavalry under the Earl of Warwick's command. Kett, having little cavalry, would have been at an immediate disadvantage and, although his cannon could have had free play over the entire field, it is difficult to see the attraction for the rebels in fighting on Dussindale.

The contemporary accounts of the rebellion, however, both give exactly the same reason for the rebels choosing Dussindale as their final battle ground. Both Neville and Sotherton record that the rebels were persuaded to fight on the dale by an ancient prophecy that promised them victory. The prophecy said:-

'The country gruffes
Hob, Dob and Hick
With clubs and clouten shoon
shall fill Dussindale with blood
of slaughtered bodies soon'

Kett and the rebels are supposed to have believed that the prophecy promised them victory if they fought at Dussindale and so, on the night of the 25th\26th of August, it was to Dussindale that the rebels marched.

Once established on the dale the rebels began to dig in. According to Sotherton the rebels *'had devysid trenches and stakes wherein they and theyrs were intrenchid and set up great Bulwarks of defence before and abowte and placid their ordinance all abowt them'*. These defences would, no doubt, have compensated for the unsuitability of the ground for infantry facing cavalry had they had a chance to finish them but it appears that Warwick moved so quickly after the rebels that they were caught before their bulwarks were fully built.

As the sun rose on the morning of Tuesday the 26th of August the soldiers in the city were quick to notice that the rebels had departed. Having stationed look-outs in the Cathedral steeple, Warwick was at once alerted of the rebels shift in position and, thinking to catch the rebels in the open with his superior cavalry, he immediately mustered a large force and set out after the rebels. Leaving the city by St Martins gate, (or Coslany gate as it was known) that lay on the northern edge of the city, Warwick marched his force east along the walls before bearing south across Mousehold heath. Warwick soon came up with the rebels and drew up his forces to oppose them across Dussindale.

Now, with the two forces facing each other across the sun baked heathland, Warwick made one final attempt to avert the coming bloodshed. Sir Edward Knyvett and Thomas Palmer, a soldier of fortune, were sent across the dale to offer, one last time, pardon to all but the leaders if the rebel army would disband. This offer, probably couched in much the same language as the previous offer made on the hillside before Norwich, was once again rejected. Now, as Knyvett's small party made their way back across the field to the Earl's army, the last chance of peace went with them.

Although actual details of the battle of Dussindale are scarce indeed, it barely rates a mention in either Sotherton's or Neville's accounts, we do know quite a large amount about the constituent parts of the two armies that fought it. From both a military and historical perspective these details of the two armies are well worth repeating as they give an added depth to our very limited knowledge of the battle itself and, perhaps, give a vivid insight into why events turned out as they did.

The rebel army commanded by Kett and his fellow leaders was a long way from being just the rabble of peasants that it has sometimes been passed off as. With some form of military training being obligatory for all able bodied men above the age of sixteen it is likely that virtually all Kett's men had a rudimentary knowledge of warfare. With each parish being obliged to maintain a parish armoury, such as the fine example that still survives today at Mendlesham in Suffolk, it is likely that many of the rebels were equipped with reasonable quality, if outdated, arms and armour. We can see from the battle that took place through the streets of Norwich that the rebels were well equipped with archers and, although it is likely that handgunners were few and far between in the rebel ranks, these archers could be counted upon to out shoot and out distance even the most modern sixteenth century firearm.

Although the rebels seem to have possessed few mounted men they did have many thousands of infantry. However, Sotherton makes it clear that these men were, in many cases armed with little more than agricultural implements such as 'muck forks, pytch forks etc'. It must also be remembered that at this period the bill, a derivation of an agricultural implement, was still the favoured weapon of many English soldiers and it is unwise to underestimate those armed with such wickedly sharp weapons.

The one area in which Kett and his forces undoubtedly outdid their opponents was in artillery. The number of field pieces in rebel hands by the time of the battle appears to have been somewhere in the region of twenty, a considerable number for the period. They had first managed to 'confiscate' several pieces from halls and houses in the surrounding area and then, upon capturing the city for the first time, they had acquired at least seven more. When they had captured the greater part of Warwick's artillery this number was probably doubled. All these guns and their associated powder and shot appear to have been under the command of Miles the master gunner who seems to have been a professional gunner of some ability.

The one drawback to having such a large artillery train was that it is unlikely that the rebels possessed enough trained gunners to use all their cannon to best effect. To place command of a cannon in the hands of an untrained but enthusiastic volunteer was both dangerous and foolhardy and it is possible that a shortage of gunners may have been partly responsible for the rebels defeat. Had they brought all their pieces to bear on the Royal army, with sufficient powder and men to serve them, it is unlikely that Warwick's casualties would have been so light.

In truth Robert Ketts army, at least in sixteenth century terms, can be considered a formidable host. Although generally inexperienced and lacking in cavalry the army had at least a hard core of professional soldiers to guide it and what it lacked in horsemen it more than made up for in artillery power. Drawn up opposite the Earl of Warwicks meagre forces on the heath at Dussindale, Robert Kett probably had between ten and fifteen thousand armed men under his command; local men with local loyalties and the strong belief that what they were fighting for was, in the eyes of God if not the government, right and just.

In contrast the army commanded by the Earl of Warwick could be said to be the exact opposite of the force they opposed. Warwick, fearing a rebel assault during his absence from the city, had felt obliged to leave the bulk of his infantry still within the defences of Norwich. Of the approximately twelve thousand bodies at his disposal he probably had little more than half with him at Dussindale. Of these the vast majority were foreign mercenaries who acted in the role of medium and heavy cavalry and saw the plain before them as a perfect terrain for their rapid deployment.

The artillery and infantry available to the Earl, although small in number, were of the best quality to be found anywhere in England. Captain Drury and his handgunners, having already proved their effectiveness against the rebels, were joined by several other units of handgunners from the mercenary ranks. Between them they probably possessed more handguns in their small units than in the entire rebel army. These handgunners were, traditionally at the period, supported by ranks of pikemen and spearmen. These pikemen were, no doubt, drawn from the mercenary ranks, as it is recorded throughout the early sixteenth century that the pike was the favoured weapon of both the German and Swiss mercenary soldiers.

Along with the infantry went the remaining guns of Warwick's artillery train. Paradoxically, where as the rebels had too many guns and too few gunners, the Royal army, after losing many of their guns to the rebels, probably possessed far more trained gunners than they now had a use for. However, the Earl's gunners were all experienced men who could be relied upon to do their jobs efficiently even at the height of battle. In a prolonged artillery fight the Earl could rest assured that his gunners would do much more damage than the inexperienced rebels.

From Warwick's position on the dale he would have been able to clearly make out the rebels dispositions. Before him stood the bulk of the rebel infantry and, sheltering behind half finished ramparts within its centre, lay the long sleek barrels of the rebel guns. In patches, hastily erected along the rebel front, were stands of wooden stakes driven deep into the earth and sharpened to deter the cavalry. Attached to these stakes, at intervals along the front line, were the rebel prisoners; chained in place to form a human shield. In the distance, far behind the rebels front, lay a mass of sprawling baggage wagons and their horses.

Warwick no doubt drew up his forces to oppose the rebels using the tried and tested tactics of the day. On each wing he stationed his cavalry, able to either outflank the enemy or sweep together into the centre, and between these two massed bodies he positioned his infantry. The handgunners, no doubt forming the front line, were interspersed with stands of spearmen and pikemen behind whom they could shelter if threatened by an enemy advance. His artillery would be placed within this same area and would also benefit from the protection of the pikemen. Warwick himself, along with his fellow commanders, stood in the centre of his army beneath the gently fluttering Royal standard.

By the time Knyvett's party had made their laborious ways back to the Royal lines noon had already been and gone and the long hot afternoon stretched before the two waiting armies. Then, like thunder out of a cloudless summer sky, came the first harsh crump of field artillery. According to Sotherton, the rebels *'begin shot of their ordenance by their Chiefe Gunner, one Mules, and killed the horse of the standard bearer and hurt him in the legge'*. As the Royal standard fluttered down into the dry August dust, first victim to the first rebel shot, the battle of Dussindale began.

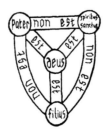

Whereof my Lord Lieuetenant, having intelligence by ye watch in Christ Church steeple, preparid himself to give battell and on Tuesday the XXVIIth day with his pwre preparid in battell arraye out att the gates callyd Gosny gates marched to them, and notwithstanding all things prest soe saving the Gentlemen with them sent Sir Edward Knyvett with others to see it they would yeelde, but of theyr obstinacy would not and to begin shot off their ordenance by their Chief Gunner, one Myles, and killed the horse of the standard bearer and hurt him in the legge, whereuppon the army shot att them and breake theyr carrage.....

Nicholas Sotherton - The Commoyson in Norfolk

Miles, the rebel master gunner, stared in abject horror at the advancing enemy. The sight of so many charging horsemen was nothing new to him, he had seen battles, sieges, sacks and skirmishes and now looked at each with the detached interest of a fellow professional. Miles' horror lay not in the hundreds of charging beasts, all topped with vicious looking horsemen, but rather in what he had done. In all his years as a gunner, through the belching flame and gouting smoke of numerous campaigns, he had never seen a first shot like it. He had targeted the Royal standard, standing as it did coldly aloof in the enemy centre, and by some freak chance his first shot had brought it fluttering to the ground.

With an unknown distance, although fairly gauged by his keen eyes, and a cold gun barrel he had hit his mark in a single shot and been rewarded by a ragged cheer from the rebel lines. At any other time and in any other place it would have been a shot to be proud of, a boast to be repeated often in the ale house, a shot in a million. Miles, however, felt only dread. A deep sick feeling in the pit of his stomach and a taste in his mouth more sour than the gunpowder. He, Miles the master gunner, had brought down the Royal standard of England, a flag he had fought under time without number, a banner he would have protected with his life and now he was the one to send it shivering down into the dust.

The rest of Miles's guns were almost as well aimed. The steel bright German cavalry had begun to advance at the trot. Trying hard to keep their horses from leaping forward, the brash Germans had come on in a straight and dreadful line, straight into the storm of iron hurled forward by the cannon. With cold barrels the shot mainly fell short, sending up great gouts of dust as they bounced once on the sun baked field and tore into the advancing horsemen. As ragged and bloody holes were ripped in the front ranks horses collided, collapsed and went sliding bloodily to the ground. Behind them more cavalry advance into the cruel nightmare only to trip and stumble on the bodies of their fallen comrades. For perhaps half a minute the scene continues as the cavalry mill in confusion and try to pass the heaps of fallen. Then like a tide they ebb and flow around the ragged red heaps and renew their advance. Battle has come to Dussindale.

Once again Miles was ready for them and, this time with warmed barrels, a second salvo tears through their ranks at waist height. A score of horses, amid a spray of sweat and blood, crash to the hard earth throwing their riders under the hooves of their unmerciful fellows. Once more the advance checks momentarily before coming on into the mouths of the guns. Now the rebel archers begin to take their toll. Armoured men and horses, making a fine target for their experienced country eyes, the archers loose their shafts into the still summer air. In the silence after the deafening bellow of the guns it sounds as if a winter flight of geese are passing over the rebels heads as the shafts take the air.

The cavalry, if they have time to listen, hear nothing. Those with the eyes to see notice something like a large cloud of silent bees growing larger by the second, a slight darkening in the perfect blue sky. Then the wicked aspen shafts are among them, piercing helmets, maiming horses and pinning the riders fine gaudy doublets to their bloody chests. Horses rear in terrified agony, try desperately to pluck the barbed shafts free and plunge and rear until their riders are unseated. The cavalry charge, in less than a minute, comes to a shocked and reeling standstill before the rebel lines. Miles, sensing a quick and easy victory, smiles to himself as he reloads his charge. Then the Royal guns reply.

Great gouts of black rimmed flame blossom forth from the Royal line as, once more, the air is split with a thunderous bellow. Solid shot passes low over the cavalry, sending more horses plunging with fear, and ploughs into the rebel lines. The Welshmen, stung by the shame of losing their guns in the narrow streets of Norwich, aim with precision. Their target is Miles and the rebel gun battery.

Most of the shots miss the battery but it only takes four of the volatile missiles to cause the damage. The first strikes the gun to Miles's left, clanging on the barrel and ringing it like a bell. The barrel, spinning backwards from its mountings, cuts down two of the gunners and shatters the trail sending a shower of deadly splinters in all directions. The splinters kill the rest of the crew outright and wound many others around them. The second ball strikes home at the far end of the line, removes a cannons wheel and spins it out of control in a devastating semi-circle. The crew are dead before they realise what has happened. The third ball lands just below a cannon in the centre of the line, bounces upwards into the belly of the beast and shatters its wooden limbs to pieces. The right wheel arcs away from the wreck, its iron rim smashing the skull of the rammer, and lands, still spinning some fifty yards away. Amazingly, apart from the rammer the rest of the crew escape unhurt.

The fourth cannon ball, landing only a scant second after the first, smashes clean into Miles' gun. Hitting the front of the axle block it shatters the axle, buckles the wheels and sends the barrel and trail sharply back into the hard packed earth. The iron wheel rim smacks aside into the brazier kept by to light the matches of the gunners and a sheet of hot coals erupts into the air. As the red hot cinders fall Miles can already see what will happen next, it is as though the world has slowed down while his mind speeds up, and he knows there is nothing he can do to stop it.

He can see the cinders falling thickly around the loaded barrel, his hand although already broken at the wrist by the initial impact, still grasps the ramrod, that lodges in the barrels mouth. He tries to move away, his mind screams at him to dive away from the barrel, but as he starts to move he sees the bright plume that erupts from the touch hole and knows he is too late.

In his detached state he does not so much hear the blast as feel it. A great wave of pressure hits him in the stomach and heaves him aside like a straw doll. The ramrod, with Miles' hand still clutching it tightly, cartwheels forward into the hot smoke. Miles, the rebel master gunner, hits the hard packed earth about ten yards from the smoking and shattered wreck of his beloved bronze gun and, still breathing, with one quarterised and blackened stump lapses into the peace brought by concussion. A child's rag doll, bloody and torn, cast aside onto the sun bleached turf.

The rebel gun battery, still wreathed in smoke, looks like a butchers shambles on Christmas Eve. Although most of the guns are still serviceable and most of the crews thankfully still alive the battery is no longer firing. The single salvo from the Royal cannons has changed it from a well ordered unit to a disorganised rabble. With Miles gone, the other captains, some bleeding, others pale and all shaken, have no one to look to for orders and guidance. Behind them the archers are screaming as they find themselves on the receiving end of a second Royal salvo.

The gun captains, disorientated by the screams and the smoke can only stand and stare as, out of the thinning smoke, come galloping the remains of the German cavalry.

The Germans, in the short minute between the first Royal salvo and reaching the rebels guns, have reorganized themselves. Their casualties were mainly among the horses and now, with fresh impetus to their charge and anger in their hearts, they bear down on the rebels guns. As they emerge from the smoke they find the line of guns arrayed before them. The older and wiser amongst them, expecting another salvo from the virtually intact battery, rein in their mounts allowing the younger, more foolhardy, riders to lead them into the rebels fire.

As they advance expecting at every second to be whipped from their saddles by a storm of flying metal, they begin to bunch together finding a mental safety in numbers. Then, almost before they realise it, they are at the guns. Around them they see the chaos caused by the Royal bombardment and, excitement and relief mixing together, they set to with their short lances to add to the slaughter. Cruel death has come to Dussindale.

Captain Drury leads his handgunners forward to support the German horse. After the first salvo from the Royal guns his position is wreathed in thick shifting smoke and with no wind to carry it away it blocks his view of the rebel lines. With drawn sword he waves his men on through the white sun sheened fog of battle each second expecting to emerge before the enemy line. Then they are clear. They walk forward and pass through the smoke and it is as if a curtain has lifted upon the world. Ahead lies another thick bank of white shifting smoke. Drury, looking around, finds himself at the head of his men and they are alone. Smoke ahead and smoke behind but they walk, calmly and orderly, across the centre of the field hidden from both armies.

Drury, knowing that this calming peace must soon end, looks around at the scenery. He takes in the bleached grass and feels the hot sun upon his helmet. He and his men are alone on a sunlit isle of peace amidst a shifting white fog. Above him, in the heated August sky, he thinks he hears the gentle song of a skylark, a sound more suited to a lovers stroll than a battles hot march. A gentle illusion of peace in the heart of the battle. Drury's calm is soon shattered as another Royal salvo passes overhead and whips ragged holes in the banked smoke before him. They are near the rebel lines and to their left they can make out dark fallen images beneath the smoke, remnants of the German charge. The sound of horses screams reach out to them and draw them once more into the world of battle, and as Drury leads his men once more into the smoke he begins a muttered prayer beneath his breath.

The German cavalry have done well this day. Their charge has taken the guns from the rebel army and now bursts through the line to wreak havoc among the ill armoured archers. Lances spear to left and right as the Germans urge their tired beasts forward and the archers, fear showing in their faces, try to throw themselves out of the path of the advancing steel points. However, the Germans alone cannot win this battle, they are too few and their charge slows as the rebel billmen turn in upon them. Now the deadly halberds of the rebels cut deep into horses flesh, swing in vicious arcs to slice men from the saddle, bring burnished steel death to the outnumbered cavalry.

Then a darkness appears in the smoke before the rebels lines, a shadow of ghosts in the white haze that transforms itself into the well ordered lines of Captain Drury and his handgunners. Death dealing angels in the mist. The rebels begin to turn from their mounted quarry, turn to face this new threat, but they are too late. Drury, calmly and efficiently, still muttering a prayer beneath his breath, gives the order and as one the handgunners level their pieces. *Our Father, which art in Heaven.* Rebel eyes show white as they find themselves staring down the two hundred deadly barrels and then, at the falling of a sword stroke, the guns give fire. *Forgive us as we forgive those who trespass against us.* Flame blossoms forth as two hundred barrels spit forth two hundred lead balls into the tight packed and unprepared rebels. *Thy Kingdom come, Thy will be done.* Death has come to Dussindale.

Now again hidden by smoke Captain Drury watches as his men reload with hasty hands and prepares to order a second volley. *Thy will be done.* His targets are no longer to be seen but all they must do is fire into the smoke. A second volley crashes out, more ragged than the first but just as deadly and then, knowing the time is right, he orders the advance. *Thy will be done.* As once more the death dealing ghosts appear through the smoke the rebels melt before them. The ground is littered the dead and dying men, all victims of Drury's fire, but before them, where there should have been thick lines of rebel bills, there is nothing but a fleeing mass. The rebels have been broken.

Captain Drury stands amidst the broken ruin of the enemy billmen and watches the rebels as they flee before his guns. He knows that the battle is won and that now no commander will be able to rally these panicked troops. His job is done but, glancing around at the sprawling bodies of his fallen enemy he feels no satisfaction. When Englishmen kill Englishmen there can be no winners, only the quick and the dead. The German cavalry have no such qualms. Seeing the fleeing mass they urge their sweating mounts into one final charge and within seconds they are amongst them. Bright steel pierces running, heaving backs, men fall beneath flashing hooves and blood runs forth on Dussindale. The battle is won but the killing is just begun.

And the same Robert Kett, and the other said traitors, on the said 27th day
of August, by favour of God, were, by the General, the most noble Earl of
Warwick, and by other faithful subjects of the same our Lord the King then
and there under the conduct of the same Earl of Warwick, honourably
subdued and conquered...
Findings against Robert Kett - November 26th 1549

By four o'clock on the afternoon of Tuesday the 27th of August the battle of Dussindale was over. The few remaining Royal guns, under expert guidance, smashed the batteries of rebel artillery and the end came quickly. Without their guns the rebels had no defence against the thousands of cavalry under the Earl of Warwick's command and found themselves at the mercy of mercenaries who, eager to earn their pay, showed no mercy. The cavalry ripped bloody holes in the rebel ranks and, in the blinking of an eye, the rebel army was transformed into a rabble of fleeing figures all eager to escape the horsemens wrath.

The destruction of the rebel artillery marked the end of any chance that Kett and his men ever had of victory. In a field perfectly suited to a large cavalry action the rebels only advantage lay in the number of field guns they possessed. Without the guns to mow down the ranks of advancing horsemen the rebels were lost. The cavalry, once through the initial ranks of the rebel lines found little opposition and simply set to killing as many of the fleeing figures as they possibly could. According to Neville one group of rebels, barricading themselves behind the baggage wagons, put up a strong resistance. Amid the jumble of carts and wagons they were free from the vengeance of the horsemen and put up a brave fight.

The Earl, no doubt happy in his victory and wishing to spare further bloodshed, ordered that the Herald should once more offer pardon to those besieged behind the wagons. These few rebels, having seen the slaughter of their comrades, were understandably suspicious and stated that they would only accept the offer of surrender if it was repeated to them by the Earl himself. Warwick, magnanimous in victory, rode forward and personally accepted the rebels surrender. With this, the last fighting came to an end and the battle of Dussindale was over.

The scale of the rebel defeat that day is well reflected in the casualty figures.

Although the original sources vary considerably upon the actual numbers it appears likely that at least three thousand men died at Dussindale. Of these the vast majority were rebels, no doubt cut down by the cavalry as they tried to flee the field. The victorious Earl of Warwick lost only seven gentlemen of quality, among whom was Robert Knyvett (cousin of Sir Edward), and some two hundred and fifty common soldiers. Warwick's troops also captured many hundreds of rebel prisoners who they marched back to the city where they were temporarily lodged within the city churches. Miraculously none of the prisoners whom the rebels had chained to stakes in front of their position were harmed during the battle and all were freed by the Royal troops without incident.

The rejoicing, either real or feigned, that greeted the Earl's re-entry into the city was almost overpowering. The city corporation, happy to be once more in control, provided two large barrels of ale for the returning soldiers that were set up at the market cross and drunk immediately. The mercers and merchants of the city were, no doubt, less ecstatic at the sudden and brutal demise of the rebel army. They were, once again, free to continue their business' but it was soon discovered that all the stock that had been carried off by the rebels and recaptured by Warwick now officially became the property of the Crown. With the drunken soldiery auctioning off their personal booty at the market cross the merchants can perhaps be forgiven the odd feeling of having been hard done by.

That night, as the tired and no doubt drunken soldiery retired to their beds, the dead were hastily buried. Tradition states that the majority were cast into pits outside the Magdalen gate for fear that, in the hot weather, their presence above ground would soon lead to disease spreading throughout the city. The gentlemen who died were laid to rest in the fine church of St Peter Mancroft.

The following morning, the 28th of August, the Earl of Warwick began to hear the cases of the many prisoners he had captured at Dussindale as well as hearing the numerous petitions from the townsfolk who were seeking compensation. Justice was swift and harsh for many of those caught in the act of rebellion. Many of the ordinary rebels were quickly despatched at the city gallows, outside the Magdalen gate, while for nine of the leading rebels, including Miles the master gunner, a more lingering fate was in store. These nine, on the direct orders of the Earl, were taken up, some say to the 'tree of reformation', and hanged. Before death seized them the nine prisoners were cut down and, while still conscious, had their bellies sliced open and their entrails pulled out; following this their heads were removed and their bodies cut into four quarters.

The heads of the nine rebels were exhibited above many of the city gates, as a warning against treason, and their disjointed bodies were dragged through the city streets before being and set up on poles 'to the terror of others'. Although we know that these nine were executed along with others outside the Magdalen gates we have no reliable source as to the actual numbers put to death by order of the Earl. Some sources, perhaps disregarding the forty nine rebels executed upon Warwick's entry into Norwich, suggest a figure as low as fifty while others, perhaps in the circumstances being a little more realistic, suggest a figure in the area of three hundred. Whatever the true figure it must be realised that the Earl was being very lenient towards his prisoners. All had been caught in the act of rebellion and were therefore guilty of treason and the punishment for treason was death.

The reasons that have been suggested for Warwick's lenience towards the rebels are twofold. Firstly, as he pointed out to the bloodthirsty and vengeful local gentry, if all the rebels were executed then the local economy, already upset by the rebellion, would suffer a dramatic labour shortage. Secondly, the Earl strongly believed there was always a place within the English legal system for mercy and forgiveness; a thought that the local landowners should have kept in mind before the rebellion began.

The following day, August 29th, the Earl, his officers and many of the leading townsfolk attended a service of thanksgiving in the church of St Peter Mancroft next to the market place. This service proved so popular that it was adopted by the city authorities as an annual event and continued for over a century. However, this was not the only lasting memorial to the Earl of Warwick within the city. During the uprising the Earl had caused his personal badge, the bear and ragged staff, to be fixed to the front of Augustine Steward's house to mark his headquarters. Other citizens, wanting to physically prove their loyalty, followed the Earl's lead and for years afterwards small bear and ragged staff symbols dotted the city. Along with these personal symbols the Earl's full coat of arms was placed alongside the Royal coat of arms above each of the city gates by a grateful city council.

The Earl remained within the city for a little over a week, finally setting out for London on the 7th of September. During his time in the city he was praised, feted and petitioned by many hundreds of the locals and was no doubt eventually pleased to be leaving with his task so successfully completed. With the rebels defeated and the majority of the countryside subdued, if not entirely quiet, the Earl now had other matters on his mind. The symptoms of rebellion had been dealt with; now it was up to Warwick to deal with the cause.

Kett, before they joyned, with V or VI rebellis fled and att Swannington,
where his horse was tirid and hee forcid to take a barne where was a cart with
corne unlading, was browt to the howse of one Mr Riches of that towne....
                    Nicholas Sotherton - The Commoyson in Norfolk

Among the many hundreds of rebel prisoners captured at the Battle of
Dussindale there was one very notable exception; Robert Kett. Accompanied by
five or six rebel horsemen Robert Kett fled the field of battle, according to
Sotherton, before the fighting actually began. This may just be a piece of
derogatory propaganda on Sotherton's part; more likely he only fled when he saw
the battle was lost. However Robert Kett did attempt to escape. Perhaps seeing
that all was lost Kett decided that his only hope lay in flight, or perhaps Kett, upon
seeing that a battle was now inevitable, a battle he had wanted to avoid, decided to
escape and disassociate himself from the coming slaughter. Whatever the truth of
the matter, and that we will never really know, Robert Kett left the area of
Dussindale and fled to the northwest.

Slipping around the northern edge of Norwich Kett rode towards the north
Norfolk coast. Here, perhaps at one of the thriving little ports such as Wells or
Cley, he probably hoped to be able to gain passage on board one of the numerous
small trading vessels and escape to the continent. However, as night began to draw
in he found himself at the small village of Swannington, a few miles south east of
Reepham. Here, traditionally in a barn by the roadside, Kett is said to have
stopped to rest his tired horse. In the barn were several local farmworkers
unloading a wagon of grain and, recognising Kett for the rebel he was, they
secured him and carried him off to the house of a local gentleman.

This gentleman, one Mr Riches of Swannington, held Kett in his custody while
he sent word to Norwich of his new prisoner. Early the next morning a troop of
Royal cavalry arrived at Riches house and took command of the prisoner who,
securely under guard, they transported to Norwich. The farmworker who had first
recognised Kett and aided in his capture was later paid a bounty of twenty
shillings by the government.

Robert Kett, the man who had been nicknamed 'captain mischief' by the local gentry, was brought before the Earl of Warwick to answer for his crimes. Warwick, rather than executing the rebel out of hand as he was empowered to do, realised that justice had not only to be done but also had to be seen to be done and ordered that Robert and his brother William should both be transported to London. Once within the capital they were to be tried in a public court of law where the whole country could witness the results of their imprudent actions.

Robert and William Kett returned to London in the train of the Earl of Warwick and by the 9th of September were both safely lodged within the confines of the Tower of London. Here, within the stark walls of England's strongest fortress the pair languished for over six weeks until, on November the 23rd, a writ was finally issued for their trial. Those six weeks of captivity may have been tedious for the Ketts but for England they were a time of intense activity. The rebellion in the west was finally ended, uprisings in the midlands suppressed and Lord Protector Somerset overthrown. When the 'great council' finally issued the order for the Ketts trial it was a council now headed by the Earl of Warwick himself.

The writ appointed six judges to try the two brothers and called upon a jury of twelve to consider, in the King's court of Chancery, the charges of treason against the two men. Finally, on November the 26th, the two Norfolk men were brought before the court at Westminster. The charges, as laid down in the writ, were read to them:-

Know ye therefore, that we, fully confiding in your fidelity, indistry, and provident circumspection, according to the form of the Statute in this case made and provided, have assigned you.............the truth of the affair may be better discovered, concerning all treasond, misprisions of treason, and murders, and each of them, by..... William Kett and Robert Kett, as well within our counties of Norfolk, Suffolk and Essex, as also within the said county of Middlesex, or within any one of them, in any way had, done, perpetrated, or committed.'

Both of the brothers pleaded guilty to the charges and, offering no defence for their actions, they were both found guilty as charged and sentenced to death. The brothers were to be returned to the Tower and from there to be *'drawn through the midst of the city of London straight to the gallows at Tyburn, and on that gallows be hanged, and while yet alive, that they be cast on the ground, and the entrails of each one of them be taken out and burnt before them, while yet alive, and their heads cut off, and their bodies divided into four parts; And that the heads and quarters of each of them be placed where our Lord the King shall appoint'*. However, before the sentence was carried out its details were changed. Perhaps as a warning to the local inhabitants it was deemed that the executions should actually take place in the Ketts home county of Norfolk.

The two brothers were then transported back through the East Anglian countryside to the city they had so recently besieged. Here they were held, much as they had held their own prisoners, in the confines of Norwich castle to await their execution. Early on the morning of December the 7th Robert's older brother William was taken from the castle and transported to Wymondham. Here, where the troubles and the Ketts involvements with them began, William Kett was hung from the steeple of Wymondham abbey.

Later that same day, December 7th, Robert Kett followed his brother out of this world. Taken from his cell in the castle keep he was led up to the battlements where, with his hands secured behind him, he was hung from the walls. The Ketts were the last of the captured rebels to be executed and, with their deaths, the rebellion finally came to an end. Robert Kett's body was left hanging from a gibbet over the castle walls at Norwich for many months. This gruesome reminder of the price of treason was finally removed when, with the return of the hot weather the following year, several townsfolk complained to the council. Kett's body was finally taken down and disposed of in an unmarked grave.

The capture, confinement and final execution of Robert Kett really takes us no closer to discovering the motives behind the actions of this enigmatic man. Neither brother offered any defence for their actions during their trial and, unlike the vast majority of condemned men of the period, neither issued any statement or recantation before their executions. Had it not been for their involvement in the short summer of madness then both men would have died in the obscurity in which they had lived and history would never have remembered the name of Kett. As it now stands historians and the public alike both know the name but little else besides. We are left much as we started with the same question. Who was Robert Kett?

It is appointed unto men once to die, but after this the judgement.
Hebrews 9,27

Within two months of the Earl of Warwick leaving the city of Norwich he had managed to overthrow Lord Protector Somerset from his position of power and replace him as head of the great council and as England's foremost nobleman. Warwick, his vision perhaps slightly twisted by ambition, saw Somerset as the root cause of much of England's troubles. Having dealt with the uprisings Warwick now dealt with their cause.

For the Earl his victory at Dussindale was more than simply putting down a treasonous rebellion; it was a confirmation that Somerset was leading England to ruin and that he, the great Earl of Warwick, was the the only man who could halt that decline. On October the 14th the former Lord Protector Somerset was delivered into custody at the Tower of London. Somerset was formerly charged with thirty one articles of which, ironically, he acknowledged only twenty nine. In another part of the Tower, a short stones throw from Somerset's cell, were held Robert and William Kett.

The sudden and brutal ending of Kett's rebellion on that fine summer day in 1549 left deep wounds in the hearts and minds of many East Anglians that would take generations to heal. The betrayal, as the rebels saw it, of a popular movement concerned with only justice and good government by the bureaucratic London authorities was simply another pointer towards the unfairness of an unjust rule. The very fact that the Government felt compelled to react so harshly towards the rebels is perhaps an indication of the just nature of the rebel claims. The local governing class were corrupt and, supported by the higher ranks in society, not only attempted but succeeded in exploiting their positions and the relative weakness of the poorer classes that made up the majority of the country dwellers.

For the city of Norwich the time of the rebellion was well remembered for many years afterwards. The salvation of the citizens by the Earl of Warwick was honoured throughout the city and the Earl's personal badge, the bear and ragged staff, was to be found adorning many of the cities houses until recent centuries. In memory of their ordeal the church service of thanksgiving, held in St Peter

Mancroft church, was repeated on an annual basis for over a century after the original events.

However, not all was quite as rosy for the leading citizens of Norwich as they wanted everyone to believe. With the return of the authority of central government the accusations began to fly thick and fast. It was pointed out by many that the actions of many of the city's leading residents during the rebellion were less than praiseworthy. Wild accusations of collaboration were levelled against the city council and several were subject to dark hints of complicity in the uprising itself. The city was berated by the 'great council' for its initial weak response to the rebel threat and overall, the years immediately after the rebellion can have been less than comfortable for the city council.

Few of those closely involved with the rebellion on either side emerged from the events of that summer with much to be proud of. The city council found themselves berated by London and hated by the rebellious locals. They had survived the uprising but only at a great cost in personal dignity. Of those closely involved with the Kett administration only Mayor Thomas Codd and his deputy Augustine Steward seem to have been shown in a generous light. Codd, it was understood, had little choice in his actions and had done his best in protecting the city's interests while Steward, at least in the eyes of Sotherton and his contemporaries, was judged one of the heroes of the hour.

For many years after the revolt itself resentment bubbled just below the surface of the East Anglian society and the 'camping time', as the rebellion became known, was looked back upon with anger and regret. As time passed the lower classes began to see that their belief that the system could be altered with the assent of central government, was misguided. The numbers that began looking towards more radical solutions became larger and more influential. Fuelled by close contact with the continent and the gradual decline in the local economy East Anglia became a breeding ground for radicals and dissenters throughout the next century.

Unfortunately, the lessons that should have been learnt by both sides during the rebellion appear to have been forgotten. When, almost a century later, civil war broke out in England it was the East Anglians, under the leadership of an East Anglian squire, that finally ended the absolute rule of one 'great tyrant' and many lesser ones. The rebel blood that was spilled on Dussindale was paid for with Royal blood and Hob, Dob and Hick had their revenge.

Kett's 29 Demands

Surprisingly only one complete copy of the demands sent by Kett and his rebels actually survives to the present day. Being unique there is no way of being sure that these demands are exactly as they were when presented by the rebels to the council. The document, now in the British Library, was originally signed by Robert Kett, Thomas Codd and Thomas Aldrich. Attached to the document, by way of a prefix, were the names of those elected by the rebels as their representatives.

These names, fifty in all, are given as two members from each of twenty four of the thirty three 'hundreds' of Norfolk. A 'hundred', although dating back to before the Norman conquest, was a unit of land, varying in size, that was used until very recent centuries as an administerative division of the county. The nine unrepresented hundreds probably reflect the fact that too few people from these areas were among the rebels to deserve separate representation. The final two names listed, to make up the round fifty, are those of Kett himself, listed along with the representatives from Forehoe, and a representative from Suffolk. The demands are reproduced here in their original order and spelling.

The rebel demands

Robert Kett, Thomas Rolff, William Kett (Forehoe)
Edmond Framingham, William Tydde (North Greenhoe)
Reynold Thurston, John Wolsey (South Erpingham)
Symond English, William Pecke (East Flegg and West Flegg)
George Blomefield, William Harrison (Launditch)
Edmond Belys, Robert Sendall (Eynesford)
Thomas Prycke, Henry Hodgekins (Humbleyard)
Richard Bevis, William Doughty (North Erpingham)
Thomas Garrod, William Peter (Taverham)
Robert Manson, Robert Ede (Brothercross)
John Spregey, Eli Hill (Blofield)
John Kitball, Thomas Clerk (Walsham)

John Harper, Richard Lyon (Tunstead)
Edward Joy, Thomas Clock (Happing)
William Mow, Thomas Holling (Henstead)
John Bossell, Valentine Moore (Holt)
Robert Lerold, Richard Ward (Loddon and Clavering)
Edward Byrd, Thomas Tudenham (South Greenhoe)
Symond Newell, William Howling (Mitford)
William Heydon, Thomas Jacker (Freebridge Lynn)
Robert Cott, John Oxwick (Gallow)
William Brown, Symond Sendall (Depwade)
Richard Wright (Suffolk)

1. We pray your grace that where it is enacted for inclosyng that it be not hurtfull to such as have enclosed saffren grounds for they be gretly chargeablye to them, and that from hensforth no man shall enclose any more.

2. We certifie your grace that where as the lords of the manours hath byn charged with certe fre rent, the same lords hath sought meanes to charge the freholders to pay the same rent, contrarye to right.

3. We pray your grace that no lord of no mannor shall comon upon the comons.

4. We pray that prests frome hensforth shall purchase no lands neyther ffre nor bondy, and the lands that they have in possession may be letten to temporall men as they were in the first yere of the reign of Kyng henry the vii.

5. We pray that the redeground and medowe grounde may be at suche price as they were in the first yere of Kyng henry the vii.

6. We pray that all marshysshe that ar holden of the Kyngs majestie by ffre rent or of any other, may be ageyn at the price that they wer in the ffirst yere of King henry the vii.

7. We pray that all Bushells within your realme be of one stice, that is to sey, to be in mesure viii gallons.

8. We pray that prests or vicars that be not able to preche and sett forth the woorde of god to hys parisheners may be thereby putt from hys benyfice, and the

parisheners there to chose an other or else the pateron or lord of the town.

9. We pray that the payments of castillward rent, and blanche fferme, and office lands, which hath been accostomed to be gathered of the tenaments, where as we suppose the lords ought to pay the same to ther balyffs for the rents gatheryng, and not the tents.

10. We pray that noman under the degre of knyght or esquyer kepe a dowe howse, except it hath byn of an ould anchyent costome.

11. We pray that all ffreholders and copieholders may take the profights of all comons, and ther to comon, and the lords not to comon nor take profyghts of the same.

12. We pray that no Fteodorye within your shores shabe a counceller to any man in his office makyng, wherby the Kyng may be ttrulye served, so that a man beeng of good consyence may be verely chosyn to the same office by the comons of the same sheyre.

13. We pray your grace to take all libertie of lete into your owne hands whereby all men may quyetly enjoy ther comons with all profights.

14. We pray that copiehould land that is onresonable rented may go as it dyd in the first yere Kyng henry vii and that at the deth of a tenante or of a sale the same lands to be charged with an esey ffyne as a capon or a reasonable some of money for a remembraunce.

15. We pray that no prest shall be a chaplain nor any other officer to eny man of honor or wryrshypp but ony to be resydent uppon ther benefices whereby ther parysheners may be enstructed with the lawes of god.

16. We pray thatt all bonde men may be ffre for god made all ffre with his precious blode sheddyng.

17. We pray that Ryvers may be ffre and comon to all men for fyshyng and passage.

18. We pray that noman shallbe put by your Eshetory and Feodrie to ffynde eny office unless he holdeth of your grace in cheyff or capite above £10 a year.

19.   We pray that the pore mariners or Fysherman may have the hole profights of ther fyshyngs as purpres grampes whalles or any grett fyshe so it be not prejudiciall to your grace.

20.   We pray that evry propriatorie parson or vicar havyng a benefice of £10 or more by yere shall eyther by themselves or by some other persone teche pore mens chyldren of ther paryshe the boke called the cathakysme and the prymer.

21.   We pray that it be not lawfull to the lords of eny mannor to purchase londs frely and to lett them out ageyn by copie of court roll to ther gret advaunchement and to the undoyng of your pore subjects.

22.   We pray that no proporiatorie parson or vicar in consideration of advoyding trobyll and sute betwyn them and ther pore parishners which they daly do procede and attempts shall from hensforth take for the full contentacon of all the tenths which nowe they do receyve but viiid. of the noble in full discharge of all other tythes.

23.   We pray that no man under the degre of esquye and shall kepe any conyes upon any of ther owne frehold or copiehold onles he pale them in so that it shall not be to the comons noysoyns.

24.   We pray that no person of what estate degre or condicion he be shall from hensforth sell the adwardshyppe of eny chyld but that the same chyld if he lyve to his full age shall be at his owne chosyn concernyng his marriage the Kyngs wards only except.

25.   We pray that no manner of person havyng a mannor of his owne shall be no other lords balyf but only his owne.

26.   We pray that no lord knyght nor gentleman shall have or take in ferme any spirituall promocion.

27.   We pray your grace to gyve lycens and aucthorite by your gracious comyssion under your grett seall to such comyssioners as your pore comons hath chosyn, or to as many of them as your majestie and your consell shall apoynt and thynke mete, for to redresse and reforme all suche good lawes, statutes, proclamacions, and all other your procedyngs, whiche hath byn bydden by your justices of your peace, Shreves, Escheators, and others your officers, from your pore comons, synes the first yere of the reigne of your noble grandfather King henry the seventh.

28.   We pray that those your officers that hath offended your grace and your comons and so provid by the compleynt of your pore comons do gyve onto these pore men so assembled iiiid every day so long as they have remayned ther.

29.   We pray that no lorde knyght esquyer nor gentleman do graze nor fede eny bullocks or shepe if he may spende forty pounds a yere by his lands but only for the provicion of his howse.

By me Robt Kett   Thomas Cod
By me Thomas Aldryche

<u>Note</u>

It is interesting to note that the hundreds not represented in the list of demands drawn up by Kett and the rebels fall into two very distinct catagories. The first, and smallest group, consisting of Docking and Smethdon both lie in the extreme north western corner of the county. The second group, consisting of Clackclose, Grimshoe, Guiltcross, Wayland, Earsham, Diss and Shropham, all lie along the south and southwestern border of the county.

The potential rebels from the second group of hundreds may well have joined the other camps at either Downham Market, the Downham bridgehead at Brandon or the Bury St Edmunds camp. These three camps would have all been closer to home than the great camp at Norwich. No camp would have been nearby for the disgruntaled commoners in the north western hundreds and they may have simply deemed it too far to travel and stayed at home.

However, the one factor that both groups of hundreds share is that between them they represent the two least populated areas of the county. With the possible exception of the hundred of Diss the areas have approximately half the number of villages than comparable areas in the rest of the county. These lightly populated areas are also the parts of the county where the increase in enclosures would have been least felt and perhaps as a result the commoners saw no reason to join the uprising.

The Chamberlains Accounts

Although the whole of the rebellion is covered by the accounts written by both Neville and Sotherton both have the disadvantage of being written after the event. They attempt to relate the events surrounding the uprising as a complete narrative and, even when not actually present, they try to give a view of the whole of the rebellion. However, such accounts, invaluable as they may be, lack certain touches of detail that bring an otherwise bone dry story to life.

Luckily for readers today we do have other accounts of the rebellion which, although not originally written as histories for general publication, do shed much light on the events of 1549. Of these separate documents one of the most enlightening must be considered to be the account book of the Chamberlain of the city of Norwich.

The Chamberlain was responsible for many of the official financial accounts for the city council and, as such, kept meticulous records of all the financial transactions that took place during the period of the rebellion. Luckily the Chamberlain was not satisfied with a simple series of numbered entries in his ledgers and took the opportunity to expand upon the mundane financial records.

Of these entries in the city account books the most fascinating comes from the period of the rebels first violent entry into the city. The city council had closed the gates and prepared their defences, no small part being played by the Chamberlain himself, but had been over run by the massive rebel forces. The city guns had been captured after bombarding the rebel camp and now, with rebel troops roaming the city streets, Kett and his associates were attempting to remove the city's remaining means of defence. The Chamberlain takes up the story :-

'that the next day, being Mary Magdalen day, the Chamberlains service done the night before, and specially for making of gunshot, was betrayed by John Fyshman to traitor Kett, so that he sent to his house about LXXX men, of which number Robert Ysod (tanner), John Barker (butcher), Eschard (miller of Heigham), were chief messengers, which persons carried the Chamberlain to the Guildhall, and there took away one whole barrel of gunpowder, and a remnant of another barrel, that was left the night before, and

certain iron bullets and lead bullets that served for the iron sling① and certain more pikes that lay over the assembly chamber, and compelled him to pay for line and a 'maunde' (basket) to carry the said pilfer. 6d

Item - they came again to the Chamberlains house and took from there 120 bullets of lead that were made the night before, and also they took from him corn, paper and serpentine powder② of his own goods, to the sum of VI l odd money, and besides that, compelled him to pay for a new firkin to put in the gunshot - 5d and for line to truss and carry the pilfer with 3d

And the next day, being XXIII July a great sort of the same company with others to the number of C persons at the least, came again to the Chamberlains house and took away his own goods, 2 bows, 3 sheafs of arrows, with cases and girdles, 4 almain halberds, 2 black bills③, certain clubs and staves, 2 almain rivets as fair as any in Norwich④ and a jack of fustian⑤, and also carried him away with them to Mousehold, to have him to the tree (of reformation), for making of the forsaid gunshot....'

①   *'the iron sling'* obviously refers to some sort of catapult used to defend the city walls from attack. Its exact nature, and the use it was put to during the uprising, is unknown.

②   *'corn, paper and serpentine powder'*. Corn is the rough gunpowder used for the main charge in a handgun of the period. Serpentine powder is the finer ground powder used for priming the handgun while the paper is used for making up the individual cartridges.

③   *'almain halberds'* and *'black bills'*. Both are varieties of polearms used by the majority of Tudor foot soldiers. The blacking referred to was a chemical process to colour the surface of the metal and prevent the need for constant cleaning.

④   *'almain rivets'* were a variety of cheap and easily produced body armour that found favour throughout the early Tudor period. The rivets were of the sliding variety and meant that the armours joints could be expanded or contracted to fit people of different sizes. This meant that the armour could be produced to a standard pattern rather than having to be fitted to any one individual.

⑤   *'a jack of fustian'*. A jack, or padded jack, was a variety of cheap cloth body armour. It was constructed of layers of thick strong material, fustian in this case, that sandwiched layers of padding between them. Small metal plates were sometimes added to the padding to give the wearer extra protection.

In Rebel Footsteps

Many of the sites that are closely connected with Robert Kett and his rebellion still survive to the present day and any interested visitor needs only a little imagination to find themselves returned to the East Anglia of four hundred and fifty years ago. Although the majority of these sites are within the confines of the city of Norwich it is not exclusively so and connections with the rebellion are to be found throughout the region. For those interested in seeing these sites at first hand we have included a small selection below. However, this short list in no way covers all the sites associated with the rebellion and not all of them are open to the public so please seek the landowners permission before visiting.

Norwich

Bishops Bridge - The only surviving medieval bridge in the city, Bishops Bridge has changed relatively little since the time of the rebellion. Although the gate-house has now disappeared (as have all the original Norwich city gates) it is still possible to stand on the bridge and gaze up the hill towards the site of the original rebel camp on the heath. It was about this bridge that much of the heaviest fighting of the rebellion took place.

Bishops Gate - Originally known as 'Holmfirth' this street was the only access to the eastern side of Norwich during the rebellion and along its length much fighting took place. The western end of the street, where it curves around the Cathedral precinct, marks the spot where Northampton's friend, the unfortunate Sheffield, was brutally slain by Fulke the butcher. The site was originally marked with an 's' carved into a slab on the footpath but, at the time of the building of the new law courts and its subsequent road improvements, the slab was removed and replaced with a wall plaque. Halfway along Bishops Gate stands the 'great hospital'. It was in the meadows behind the hospital that the townsfolk established their artillery position that was over run during the first rebel assault and led to the rebels capture of at least half a dozen extra cannon.

The Cow Tower - Now in the care of English Heritage this massive tower defended the bend in the river Wensum. Originally built as a detached bastion the tower gained its unusual name from its position in the 'cowholme' pasture.

Although it appears to have played little part in the defence of Norwich during the rebellion the Cow Tower still gives a vivid impression of how much of the cities defences must have looked during the period.

Tombland - This open area of the city lies just outside the two impressive western gates to the Cathedral precincts and is an important site in terms of the rebellion. Here still stands both Augustine Stewards house and the Maids Head. Although much changed today the original Maids Head tavern occupied the same site and it was here that Lord Sheffield broke his fast on the morning of his death. A few yards away stands the impressive building constructed by Augustine Steward shortly before the rebellion. Still much as it was when first built this fine timber framed building acted as both Steward's home and shop and, during the Earl of Warwick's defence of Norwich, acted as the Royal armies headquarters.

The Cathedral - This fine Norman Cathedral saw many of the comings and goings of the various sides during the rebellion. Used by the rebels as a dry alternative to sleeping on the open heath and the Earl of Warwick's army as an observation post, the Cathedral appears to have remained undamaged during the turbulent uprising. Sitting, as it does, directly opposite Warwick's headquarters in Augustine Steward's house the look-outs in the tower could give the Earl ample warning of the rebels movements and it was from here that Warwick first received news of the rebel evacuation of their camp on Mousehold heath.

The Market Place - Although many of the surrounding buildings have altered radically during recent centuries the market place itself is much as it was at the time of the rebellion. It was here, at the now missing market cross, that the Earl of Warwick captured nearly fifty rebels during his first entry into the city. As a warning to the rest of the rebel soldiers the prisoners were executed on the spot.

St Peter Mancroft - This magnificent church, probably one of the finest in the city, was the scene of a service of thanksgiving held after the defeat of the rebel army at the battle of Dussindale. The service was attended by the Earl and his officers as well as many of the leading citizens of Norwich. The service was then repeated annually for over a century to commemorate the city's salvation.

The Guildhall - Originally built in the fifteenth century the Guildhall was one of the centres of the city's administration during the rebellion. Upon the rebels first assault and capture of the city the Guildhall was broken open and the arms and ammunition stored there were confiscated for rebel use. It was here also that Northampton, upon entering the city, first met the surviving and loyal city councillors. Now the city's main Tourist Information Centre, the Guildhall shows few signs of its turbulent past.

The Castle - Originally built by the Normans the castle still dominates the Norwich skyline. On the castle ditches, at the foot of the great rectangular keep, the city authorities first established their artillery in an attempt to bombard the rebel camp on Mousehold heath. The keep was later used by both sides as a prison and it was here that Robert Kett and his brother William were lodged prior to their executions. Robert Kett was put to death here on the 7th of December 1549 and his body remained hanging from the battlements for several months afterwards. The keep today houses the city's main museum and a plaque now adorns the wall by the entrance commemorating the events of that summer long ago.

The Boom Towers - At the southern end of King Street lie the largest and best preserved sections of the old city's defences. To the east, by Carrow Bridge, stand the stark remains of the Boom Towers. The boom, consisting of two large chains of 'Spanish iron', was operated by a windlass in one of the towers and allowed the city authorities to control the river traffic. Following the line of the city wall west from the boom towers are two well preserved towers linked by almost complete stretches of curtain wall. Together they give a vivid impression of how the defences of Norwich must have looked at the time of the rebellion.

Beyond The City Walls

Dussindale - The actual site of the final confrontation between the rebel forces and the Earl of Warwick's Royal army was, for many years, a mystery. However, in recent years, Anne Carter discovered a map of 1718 that marks a place called 'Dussing's Deale'. It appears likely that this is the position of the rebels final stand. Today the area lies in the eastern outskirts of the city beneath a new housing estate on Dussindale road and St Andrews hospital at Thorpe. Although this recent development has obscured the battlefield it has meant that once again the name of Dussindale can be found on a map of Norwich.

Wymondham - The pretty little market town of Wymondham stands some ten miles south west of the city of Norwich and it is here that the rebellion can be considered to have begun in earnest. The home town of the Kett family and the scene of the original gathering of the rioters the town has many reminders of the events of that turbulent summer of 1549. The imposing bulk of Wymondham Abbey still stands and it was disputes over this building that first led to the feud between Robert Kett and John Flowerdew that came to a head during the uprising. Wymondham was also the scene for one of the final, and most tragic, acts of the rebellion. It was here, from one of the Abbey towers, that William Kett, Robert's older brother, was finally put to death on the 7th of December 1549. Although much of the early town was destroyed in a devastating fire in 1615 it is today a charming place to visit with many fine buildings of interest.

Kett's Oak (Hethersett) - Halfway between Wymondham and the village of Hethersett, the one time home of the troublesome John Flowerdew, stands a majestic oak known locally as Kett's Oak. It is said that it was beneath this very tree that Robert Kett addressed his followers and roused them to march against Norwich. Although it is unknown how much truth actually lies behind the tale the oak has been well tended over the years and although now decayed with age a new tree has been planted close by. Grown from an acorn from the original tree the new oak should carry on the tradition for centuries to come.

Swannington - About ten miles north west of the city of Norwich sits the small village of Swannington. It was here, in a barn traditionally sited in Kett's Lane, that Robert Kett was finally captured after the battle at Dussindale. Stopping to rest his tired horse he was recognised by some local farmhands and soon taken into custody. The house of Mr Riches, where Kett was held prisoner for a short time, no longer exists but it seems likely that it occupied the same site as the later built Swannington Hall.

Kett's Oak (Ryston) - Just to the south east of Downham Market lies the parish of Ryston and here, in private parkland, stands another old tree known as Kett's Oak. Traditionally the gathering place for the rebels in the Downham area the tree has also been known as the 'oak of reformation'; the name given to the original tree on Mousehold heath where the rebels held there meetings.

Bury St Edmunds - Although the actual site of the rebel camp at Bury St Edmunds is no longer known it is believed to have been the major rebel centre for west Suffolk. Although little is known about the rebel activities in the area the camp is believed to have been abandoned as contingents of the Royal army advanced towards it from London. Today the town houses many fine museums and sites of interest.

Melton - The largest of all the rebel camps outside Norwich was situated at Melton just outside Woodbridge in Suffolk. Although originally camping at Ipswich the rebels moved to Melton to associate their rule with that of the old 'liberty of St Audrey' that was based there. Although little is known of the camp it is believed to have been almost as large as the gathering at Norwich and to have established its rule over much of the area. The Melton camp was disbanded with little or no bloodshed after the destruction of the camp at Norwich, and many of the participants afterwards felt that they had been betrayed and bought off with false promises.

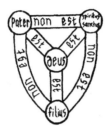